C000184203

Chilling True Tales of Old Preston

K. A. Johnson

OWL
BOOKS

First published September 1990
Reprinted January 1991
Owl Books,
P.O. Box 60,
Wigan WN1 2QB

The copyright content of this book is held by K.A. Johnson
and Owl Books and may not be reproduced in any form
without prior written permission from the publishers.

ISBN 0 9514333 4 2

Set in Cheltenham 10.5 point on 12.25 point
via DTP with 800 d.p.i. laser printer

Designed and typeset by Graphic Design, Wigan.
Printed and bound in Great Britain.

Like his predecessors, as far back as he can trace, Keith Anthony Johnson is a Prestonian. Born in the post-War baby boom, he was educated initially at St. Augustine's Roman Catholic School, before completing his studies at Harris College.

For many years he has had an avid interest in local history and in particular the lives of Preston people of a bygone age and is a member of the Lancashire Authors' Association.

Married with two young sons, he lives and works in the town as an engineering designer.

ACKNOWLEDGEMENTS

I am indebted to local newspaper journalists, of a bygone age, particularly of the *Preston Chronicle, Preston Guardian* and *Lancashire Daily Post* (the forerunner of today's *Lancashire Evening Post* whose detailed news coverage of events so long ago have helped to make this book possible.

I acknowledge the assistance given to me by the consistently courteous and helpful staff of Harris Reference Library and also Lancashire County Council for kind permission to photograph the interior of Lancaster Castle.

INTRODUCTION

IN Anthony Hewitson's 'History of Preston', published in 1883, a local chronology table lists the events that took place in the township. One of the events recorded was the execution, at Lancaster, of Jane Scott, of Preston, for poisoning her mother. This occurrence led me on a trail of violence and its attendant disregard for the sanctity of human life in the town during the 19th century and early part of this century.

At the beginning of the 19th century, the population of the Borough of Preston was just over 12,000. Some 40 years later this figure had increased to over 40,000 and by the time Hewitson completed his book, over 97,000 people populated the streets of the town. Preston had become a town dominated by the cotton industry and one influenced by the great developments of the Industrial Revolution.

The railway age was upon us and the canal system was heavily used for the transportation of goods. Workers were housed in rows of endless terraces facing cobbled streets. Few had the comforts we now take for granted; their world was harsh, strict and cruel. Poverty was endemic; there was no welfare state to ease the suffering of the less fortunate. For the downtrodden who came by hard times through injury or age, the indignity of the workhouse was the only form of shelter followed by an eventual pauper's grave.

Following the abolition of beer duty tax in 1830, rapid increases in the numbers of licensed premises took place. From 1830, in a period not exceeding 50 years, Preston's alehouses increased from 70 to 460. Some 231 of these being classed simply as beerhouses. In many cases they were no more than a converted front parlour serving ale brewed by the host. After a long day in the factory the choice for many was a stark one — either a visit to the alehouse or a return to the flag-floored, damp squalor that was home.

It was against this backcloth that the temperance movements and associated burial societies emerged, in an attempt to educate the population in ways of leading a better and more fulfilling existence. The local temperance leader during the 19th century was a man named Joseph Livesey. Dubbed 'The Moral Reformer', he was a man who cared so much for his fellow human beings that he produced a regular publication titled: 'The Struggle', in which he attempted to lead people away from the perils of drink.

Employees in the cotton trade often felt bitter about the primitive conditions in which they lived. By the middle of the 19th century there were no less than 75 cotton spinning and manufacturing establishments surrounded by primitive terraced houses. The cumulative effects of insanitary conditions and unbridled drinking, caused the town to have the highest infant mortality rate in the country. One correspondent of the age stated that the men of Preston "were old at forty".

Unions were then in their infancy and the controllers of industry appeared to have mainly uncharitable dispositions. Strike action gained little reward and more often than not a dejected workforce returned to a reduction in wages, or were simply starved back after an enforced lock-out.

The church of the 19th century attempted to be the fabric of society and many of our present-day churches had their foundations laid in this period, particularly those dissenting churches of the established Church of England. The churches strived to give the poor an opportunity to gain some education. At the turn of the century about 10,000 children regularly attended Anglican and non-conformist Sunday Schools in the town.

With the rapid increase in population came the need for additional policing. Gradually constables became a welcome and familiar sight on the streets of the Borough. In 1832 just half- a-dozen officers were employed; by the middle of the 19th century this had increased to 15. Disorderly conduct came mainly at night, when the factories emptied and with this in mind, a dozen officers were then employed on night duty in the dimly lit streets.

The increased population led to increased crime and by the 1880s one hundred constables were engaged in the Borough. They had none of the sophisticated equipment used by today's Force, yet successfully managed to maintain law and order.

* * * *

The tales that follow recall the actions of simple folk trapped in a cruel environment. Their privations often caused mental instability which in turn often led to violence. Others consumed by passion, jealousy or other human failings committed acts which were tragic in the extreme.

Drink related crimes abounded, as did crime due to the bitterness created by intolerable living conditions. Inevitably robbery, forgery, rape, suicide and murder all-too-frequently occurred in the Preston of old.

Justice seemed harsh. The criminal of the 19th century faced the very real threat of the hangman's noose. Punishment was often swift. A condemned man of the 1820s was not allowed to see the sun set for a second time before his execution took place.

Many wrongdoers of Victorian-era Preston faced the ordeal of trial at Lancaster Assizes. There the Grand Jury presided and justice was meted out with little compassion. The alternatives to execution were 'Transportation For Life' or 'Penal Servitude'. Transportation did not mean a free ticket to a new life across the seas, but a number of years in chains followed by several more enduring hard labour.

The crimes I have catalogued are typical of those of a town caught-up in the momentum of the Industrial Revolution and reflect the hardships our forefathers had to endure. I believe it is not for us to condemn the criminals of the 19th century, but rather to try to understand the society in which they lived. Like their victims, all were often trapped in circumstances beyond their control; they and their victims deserve our pity and sorrow for the suffering they had to endure.

K.A. Johnson, 1990

The imposing 'John O'Gaunt' Gateway to Lancaster Castle, was seen for the first and last time by many Preston wrong doers of the 18th and 19th centuries.

Facing: *Map of Preston 1865*

CONTENTS

Jane Scott Accused of "Paracide"

"PARACIDE — Man and wife poisoned by arsenic supposed to have been administered by their own daughter", so read the front page headline in the *Preston Chronicle* on 19th May, 1827.

The report went on to recount the particulars of the dreadful catastrophy. The victims in the torrid affair were man and wife, John and Mary Scott.

The couple kept a small shop in Bridge Street and had living with them a daughter named Jane. She was 21-years-old and well known for her "depraved and dissolute conduct" and over the years had caused them much anxiety. She was already the mother of two illegitimate children, the last of which had died about two months before the incident. The child's death had been so sudden that suspicions were now entertained that the daughter may have also contrived to that death.

On Monday evening, 14th May, 1827, it was reported that the parents of the girl had been taken ill after eating part of some porridge that the daughter had prepared for their supper. Within a short time means were taken to revive them but the poison, mixed with the porridge, was too powerful. The mother died at about three o'clock the following morning and her husband passed away a couple of hours later.

Jane Scott, their daughter, was subsequently charged with the murder of both parents and sent for trial at Lancaster Assizes, where she was firstly tried with the crime against her father, who had been well-known as a traveller for the cotton industry.

Amazingly, despite what seemed overwhelming evidence against her, Scott was acquitted by the jury. Mr. Justice Bayley then gave her the option of being tried upon the second charge immediately, or of waiting until the next Assizes. She chose the latter and towards the end of March, 1828, she appeared on the charge of murdering her mother.

Once again Mr. Justice Bayley was assigned to the trial but felt some repugnance at having the girl before him again on a similar charge, he prevailed upon Mr. Baron Hullock to take the case on this occasion.

As the jury was about to be sworn in the prisoner requested that "no person from Preston or the neighbourhood be put upon it". Once selected the jury was then instructed to dismiss from their minds any previous knowledge they may have had concerning the case.

The trial followed much the same pattern as the first one had and evidence was stacked-up against the girl. A druggist from Preston recounted how two months before the death of her parents, the accused had visited his shop for a quarter-of-an-ounce of arsenic to poison rats. On two further occasions she returned for more arsenic saying that she had not quite destroyed all the rats. The last occasion was just three days before her parents' death. At the time the druggist warned her that it was a deadly poison. Her answer was that she intended to put some into whitewash to destroy bugs.

On the night of the deaths it was stated that local surgeon, Dr. Brown, had attended the unfortunate couple. He recalled how he had instructed the accused to retain the pan which contained the remains of the porridge but when he later enquired for the pan it had been washed out and all the porridge removed.

An acquaintance of hers, George Richardson, told how a week before the death of her parents, Jane Scott had talked to him about marriage. When he told her he had no money to buy furniture, she had told him that soon she would have everything they needed and also told him that her father would be signing over whatever they needed. She also said that if she had a mind to, she could have whatever she wanted.

Towards the end of the trial the defence attempted to call into evidence the verdict of acquittal from the previous Assizes, but this proposal was dismissed by Mr. Baron Hullock, who emphasised that she was being tried on this indictment only.

The jury retired and deliberated for some twenty minutes before returning to pronounce a "Guilty" verdict. An awful silence then fell upon the Court and the prisoner realising her situation, was greatly affected. She appealed to His Lordship to extend his mercy by 'transporting' her and thus sparing her life.

His Lordship then addressed her stating it was out of his power to alter the sentence of the law fixed as a punishment for the crime. He then announced that she "be taken to the place from where she came, and from there to the place of execution on Saturday next, and there hang by the neck until dead, and afterwards the body be taken down and dissected and anatomized". She wept in great agony while the judge addressed her, and with a slow and tottering pace left the bar.

During the final week of her life she confessed to the murder of both her parents and her two children. She also entered into particulars implicating other persons in her wicked crimes, but little countenance was given to the word of such a reckless creature. She attributed her course of criminal excess to an early departure from the paths of virtue, having borne a child when she was only sixteen years of age. She also revealed how she had long carried out a system of robbery upon her parents, the proceeds of which she had spent amongst the most abandoned company she could meet.

Many persons from Preston who wished to witness her execution on March 22nd, 1828 set off for Lancaster in the middle of the night. The churchyard and every place which afforded a view of the scaffold was crowded to excess. Indeed according to the oldest inhabitants of Lancaster the crowd was greater than on any similar occasion. At midday the execution party appeared and positioned themselves around the scaffold. Shortly aftwards the condemned woman appeared and walked to the gallows supported by two female attendants. To all appearances she seemed more dead than alive and opened her eyes

Edward Barlow, Hangman

Edward Barlow, commonly known as "Old Ned" was said to be a greater villain than many he "turned off" as hangman at Lancaster Castle.

Barlow led a wretched life. He was reputed to have been sentenced to death for horse stealing, then a capital offence, and was twice sentenced to transportation. Instead he received paroles for his crimes and allowed to continue as hangman.

On 19th April, 1817, he officiated as executioner to nine at the same time. Five of the victims were under 20 years of age. They all hung so close together that they jostled one another on the drop - a sight "harrowing to the last degree".

He was described as a man who had little consideration and sympathy for his victims and was on many occasions pelted with various foul missiles. There were few homes in which he was permitted to enter.

For all this he maintained his position as hangman with little interruption for a period of 30 years during which time he "turned off" 131 victims.

He lived to be an old man and died in the castle.

only as she reached the outside of the castle; she did not appear conscious of her fate.

Once on the scaffold, the executioner slipped the noose around her neck and drew the cap over her face. The chaplain read part of the burial service as the two women supported her. She then fell back to the extremity of the rope, with her face to the crowd and was launched into eternity.

The execution of Jane Scott was carried out by Edward Barlow, commonly called 'Old Ned'. A Welshman, Edward Barlow was said to be as great a villain as any he put to death.

Postscript on Jane Scott

The tale of Jane Scott when examined from a contemporary viewpoint suggests she was in fact a cripple and had to be wheeled to her execution in a chair which visitors to Lancaster Castle can see, though the reports of her trial reveal no such disability. She was also said to have suffered from fits. It is known that two female attendants had to support her prior to the execution and her weak condition could have been attributed to the fact that from the day preceding her trial, to the time of her execution, she took no food of any kind.

By grim twist of fate it is reputed that Scott's skeleton eventually found its way back to Preston. The wired-up bones were apparently purchased by a Dr. Thomas Monk, who himself, stood on trial at Lancaster Assizes in 1858. In later years another Preston man

The death chair on view at Lancaster Castle. It is said to have been used to 'transport' Jane Scott to the gallows

4

bought the skeleton at an auction for a few shillings and took it to his shop in Walker Street. There it was kept in a long coffin-shaped box in an upright position just behind the kitchen door. On the box lid was said to be a plate bearing the name 'Jane Scott'.

In later years the shop became empty and was boarded up. The shop's owner recalled returning to the premises one day and finding the bones scattered in the backyard, after children had apparently broken into the premises.

A Dog Called 'Morgan' Finds a Savage Killer

ON 7th April, 1876, posters appeared on hoardings in Preston, announcing the shocking murder of a seven-year-old girl, by the name of Emily Holland, in Blackburn, some ten days earlier. The posters offered a reward of £100 for the discovery of her killer and a subsequent conviction.

The savage crime had been discovered following the finding of the legs and trunk of the little girl in the outlying districts of Blackburn. A connection with Preston was made because of the fact that both the legs and trunk had been wrapped in back issues of the *Preston Herald* newspaper.

Various witnesses had testified to seeing the girl in the company of a man on the afternoon of her disappearance and as a result, a man described as a local tramp had been taken into custody; but the police were far from convinced of the man's guilt and the search was still being continued for the missing remains of the child.

Among the many people in Preston who had read the poster, was a printer named Peter Taylor. Like many he had been appalled to learn of the dreadful killing and with the reward very much in mind, he arrived in Blackburn the following Sunday. With him were two dogs — one a half bloodhound and spaniel and the other a clumber spaniel. After discussions with the chief constable of Blackburn, Taylor, along with his dogs and police detectives went to the spot at Bastwell, where the trunk of the body had been found to see if any scent of the remaining portions of the body could be found. The dogs did not appear to scent anything and so disappointedly, all returned to Blackburn.

The chief constable then decided that the dogs should be taken to the lock-up shop of a local barber, named William Fish, of whom they were suspicious. The premises and the home of the man were both in nearby Moss Street. In the company of Fish and his wife the party all went along to the barber's shop where they commenced their search. The officers and the dogs went upstairs, where the bloodhound at once scented up the chimney of the front room. Taylor put his hand up the chimney and pulled down from a recess of the draughty hole, a child's skull and other portions of a child wrapped in a paper and covered with blood.

The skull was blackened and it was evident that the head had recently been burnt. Confronted with the finds, 26-year-old Fish made no reply. News of the discovery spread rapidly and soon a large crowd had assembled in the vicinity of the premises.

Fortunately the timely arrival of the chief constable and other police officers enabled the removal of Fish to the police lock- up, and away from a possible lynching by the crowd.

Masthead of The Preston Herald *of November, 1875, a copy of which was used to wrap the legs and trunk of the unfortunate child, Emily Holland.*

By the time the Blackburn barber appeared before the magistrates, a great deal of conclusive evidence had been gathered to indicate his guilt. Part of the girl's clothing had been found on his premises, and in the shop were found a quantity of *Preston Heralds*, the only copies missing were the editions which corresponded with those used to wrap the dismembered body. The evidence submitted, the chief constable then produced a confession made by Fish a few days after his arrest:

Chief constable Potts then submitted the following statement made by the prisoner:

Police Office, Town Hall, Blackburn.

17th April, 1876, 4-40 p.m.

Statement made by William Fish, who has been this day brought before the magistrates on the charge of the wilful murder of Emily Holland, on the 28th March, 1876.
"I told Constable William Parkinson that I had burnt part of the clothes, and put the other part under the coals in my shop; and I now wish to say that I am guilty of the murder. I further wish to say that I do not want the innocent to suffer. At a few minutes after five o'clock in the evening, I was standing at my shop door, in Moss Street, when the deceased child came past. She was going up Moss Street. I asked her to bring me one half-ounce of tobacco from Cox's shop. She went and brought it to me. I asked her to go into my shop. She did. I asked her to go upstairs, and

she did. I went up with her. I tried to abuse her, and she was nearly dead. I then cut her throat with a razor. This was in the front room, near the fire. I then carried the body down stairs into the shop; cut off her head, arms and legs; wrapped up the body in newspapers, on the floor; wrapped up the legs also in news-papers, and put those parcels into a box in the back kitchen. The arms and head I put in the fire. On the Wednesday afternoon, I took the parcel containing the legs to Lower Cunliffe; and, at nine o'clock that night, I took the parcel containing the body to a field, at Bastwell and threw it over the wall. On Friday afternoon I burnt part of the clothing.

On the Wednesday morning I took a part of the head which was unburnt, and put it up the chimney, in the front bedroom.

I further wish to say that I did it all myself; no other person had anything to do with it.

The foregoing statement has been read over to me, and is cor-rect. It is my voluntary statement, and, before I made it, I was told that it would be taken down in writing and given in evi-dence against me.

        (Signed)   WILLIAM FISH

        (Witnesses)   ROBERT EASTWOOD
                                        Superintendent

                                        JOSEPH POTTS
                                        Chief Constable

As the inquest drew to a close the jury returned a verdict of Wilful Murder against Fish and indicated that the vagrant, Robert Taylor, originally suspected of the crime should be released. Fish was taken to trial at the next Liverpool Assizes.

On the release of Robert Taylor, the tramp, wrongly suspected of murder, a large demonstration took place outside the Town Hall in favour of the tramp. He was raised shoulder-high by the crowd, who offered him drink and food in abundance.

The bloodhound, which had been instrumental in the apprehension of Fish soon became the focus of public interest. The dog's name was Morgan and in fact was said to be the property of James Parkinson, a lamp and oil merchant of Church Street, Preston, who had put it in the care of the Taylors on account of the dog's growing eccentricity.

Of mixed breed — retriever and bloodhound being the prominent strains — the animal had at one time been extremely obedient, fetching his master's hat, handkerchief or any named article when instructed. For a while, however, the animal had been quite vicious and without the slightest provocation threatened to bite any ill-dressed or poor-looking person.

The dog was from then on in great demand and offers came in from various sources for the animal to appear in public. One offer was made for £25 per week for appearances and another, to gain ownership, was for over £200. Considering the dog had last changed hands for just £1, was an indication of its new-found fame.

Within days, the dog became the centre of an ownership row with Thomas Bailey, landlord of the York Castle public house in Adelphi Street, Preston. Bailey claimed that in fact Morgan belonged to him. A letter to this effect was written by Thomas Bailey and it appeared in the *Preston Chronicle* on 22nd April, 1876.

To the Editor of *The Preston Chronicle*.

19th April, 1876.

"Sir, — I shall be obliged if you will insert the following in your next issue, as to the ownership of the dog 'Morgan', which has been the means of finding out the Blackburn Murderer. I am the owner of the dog 'Morgan', and have been for the last seven months past, and I cannot understand Mr. Parkinson wishing the public to believe that he is the owner of the dog. Trusting to your kind insertion of the above, I am yours truly,

THOMAS BAILEY,
York Castle, Adelphi Street, Preston.

The letter was followed by the appearance of Bailey and Parkinson at Manchester Assizes in July, 1876, with Bailey claiming that Parkinson had taken the dog from his possession. He claimed that the animal had spent some time at the public house and had, in its younger days, been in the ownership of the accused, but being difficult to control he had returned it to its original owner, a Mr. Spencer. The landlord's claim was that he had never relinquished right to the dog's ownership and that subsequently, Mr. Spencer, could not have sold the animal to another party.

At the end of lengthy proceedings, during which the dog's obvious value for its appearances for commercial gain was apparent, it was decided by the jury to find in favour of James Parkinson. He left the court the officially recognised owner of Morgan, the dog everyone wished to see.

One week later it was the turn of William Fish to take centre stage as he appeared at the Liverpool Assizes. The trial was a sorry affair and the jury soon reached the conclusion of "Guilty".

His Lordship donned the black cap and pronounced sentence of death on the man who had outraged, murdered and dismembered the body of an innocent child.

Three weeks later, along with another convicted murderer named Richard Thompson, he was executed at Kirkdale gaol, Liverpool, one Monday morning in August, 1876.

Postscript on a Dog Called 'Morgan'

Almost a year later, Peter Taylor, who had been instrumental in solving the crime and responsible for the fame of Morgan, received a reward of £100 for his part in the conviction of Fish.

A Most Peculiar Parcel

ON the night of 23 November, 1875, an 18-year-old factory worker from Walton-le-Dale named Margaret Hunter, went to Preston Railway Station with a soap box in her possession. Attracting the attention of a railway porter, the young lady asked him to arrange for its transportation to Liverpool on the 6.35 p.m. train. The box was clearly marked for the attention of a Mr. Williams, Liverpool, and the understanding was that he would collect it from the station.

When the train reached Liverpool, the railway guard, as was his duty, deposited the package on the platform. It was collected by an inspector and he took it to the left luggage department of the station, where the clerk of the department placed it on a shelf.

A few minutes later the clerk heard a muffled cry and his attention was drawn to the soap box. He carefully untied the cord that bound it and lifted the lid to reveal a small child which lay on a small piece of carpet. Carefully removing the infant from its cramped position, he moved it close to the fire to try to remedy its cold condition.

By now it was about 8.30 p.m. The local constable was alerted and the child was then taken to the workhouse, where it was fed. The infant was in a very emaciated and feeble condition and despite the attention of the workhouse staff, it died some 11 days later.

The result of the actions of Margaret Hunter on that November evening led to her appearance in March, 1876, at Livepool Assizes. She was brought before Mr. Baron Huddleston charged with the manslaughter of her child, Francis Hunter, by sending him in a soap box from Preston to Liverpool. The child was about one month old when it made its fatal journey; its unmarried mother having bore him at Accrington.

She had carefully concealed the birth from her mother, who she normally resided with. Eventually her mother did get her to admit that she had given birth to a child, and for a few days before Margaret Hunter finally decided to send the infant to Liverpool, all lived together at the family home.

As the mystery was unravelled it became clear that the mother of the child believed that what she had done had been in the best interest of the child. She had remembered the Williams family with great affection, when as a child herself, the family had been very fond of her.

Unbeknown to her mother, Hunter had prepared the unusual package and took it to the Railway Station. She claimed that at the same time, she had written to Mrs. Williams, asking her to take charge of the infant. Both the parcel and the letter, however, had no detailed address on them and subsequently did not reach their intended destination.

There was much speculation as to whether the letter had in fact been sent and in any case the Williams family had long since moved away from the area.

The daughter had told her mother that the child had gone back to Accrington, but as news of the 'baby in the soap box' spread, she became suspicious of her daughter's actions. A few days elapsed before her daughter finally admitted her action and once she did so, the pair of them went to Liverpool to see the infant.

At that stage the child was in the care of the workhouse and although in a delicate state, was still alive. The mother then revealed the identity of the child and as a result her daughter, Margaret Hunter was taken into custody.

The frail condition of the infant was revealed by medical experts at the trial and the opinion was that it would have died irrespective of the train journey. Question was: 'Did the actions of the mother accelerate the end of the child's life'.

As the proceedings drew to a close His Lordship pointed out that from the evidence submitted there was no suggestion of negligence on the part of the prisoner.

It would appear, he suggested, that she had done a very foolish thing in sending the child to Mrs. Williams in Liverpool, even if she believed that she would adopt it. He also went on to point out that had the prisoner put the child in the box, fastened it down, and despatched it to a purely fictitious address then such an act would almost amount to murder.

The foreman of the jury, after consultation with the other members, announced that in their opinion there was not sufficient evidence upon which to convict and therefore their verdict was one of "Not Guilty".

It was then stated there was another indictment for exposing the child to danger. This was no longer thought to be applicable and His Lordship ordered the prisoner to be discharged.

The Double Life of Mayor Birchall

THOMAS Birchall was a solicitor with his father's firm and he resided at the sixty-five acre Ribbleton Hall, later to become the site of the Moor Nook School. One of the Birchall's clients was the wealthy Rev. Richard Rothwell and it was through him that Birchall met his future wife, Mary Rothwell, the vicar's niece.

Thomas Birchall was 24-years-old in 1834, when he married Mary, who was then 21. When he was 38-years-old he became a Tory councillor and within two years he was elected Mayor of Preston.

At this time little was seen of his wife as the Mayoress and Mayor Birchall often attributed her absence to the delicate state of her health.

In 1857, Alderman Birchall became senior partner in the family firm. Now aged 48 and seeking more attractive interests, he quit his council duties to become Colonel of the newly-formed 21st Lancashire Artillery Volunteers. By then he had acquired considerable wealth due to a growing business and so he decided to have his Ribbleton Hall home rebuilt. The new larger Gothic-style mansion had 14 bedrooms, five entertaining rooms, a drawing room, billiard room, conservatory, vine and peach houses and stables.

Much of his time was spent away from his mansion, where his wife believed him to be on Court duty in Manchester. Alas, he was having a love affair with a Preston woman, who he had 'set-up' in a beautifully furnished lodge in Manchester. His own marriage childless, this woman bore him a son and later she died giving birth to a daughter.

Shortly afterwards, Birchall engaged another woman to take care of his children and in due course she too became his mistress and was well cared for. About this time his wife's wealthy uncle died and Birchall, who had always been trusted by him, made out his will for him.

Birchall decided to make himself sole executor and trustee, transferring the vicar's shares to his own name and taking £45,000 from the estate which should have been left to his wife, Mary. He told his wife that he had made his own will and that he had left the whole of his estate to her.

Somehow he kept up the pretence of being the devoted husband until his death. In May, 1878, his wife received a telegram informing her that her husband had died suddenly at the home of a friend.

Regarded as a benevolent man and a pillar of society, the former Mayor of Preston — who had provided soup kitchens for hungry cotton workers — was given an impressive funeral at St. Leonard's Church, Walton-le-Dale.

It was only after the funeral it was revealed that the will Birchall had given to his wife, had been revoked by a later will he had made, in favour of his mistress and his children.

Until then, Mary Birchall had known nothing about her husband's double life, which naturally came as a tremendous shock. In the will he left his mistress the Manchester lodge together with an allowance, plus Mary's personal jewellery, when she died. His wife was to get an annuity of £400 per year and £10,000, which belonged to her already

Thomas Birchall's Ribbleton Hall mansion which was demolished in 1949. The site is now occupied by Moor Nook School.

Reproduced by kind permission of the Lancashire Evening Post.

as part of the £45,000 her late uncle had intended her to have in his will. She was to be allowed to continue to reside at Ribbleton Hall and after her death the estate was to go to Birchall's eldest or surviving child, along with a sizeable portion of the remaining fortune.

Not surprisingly, Mary decided to contest the will, but as the Law stood, women in the marriage state, assumed only the legal rights of an infant. Property passed to the husband's possession and without his consent a wife could not make a will.

The case was heard by Chancery and adjourned three times without settlement. The Judge understood Birchall's widow being angry, commented that her husband's life had been one long swindle. A couple of years later when the son became 21, Mrs. Birchall decided to end the deadlock by agreeing on an out-of-court settlement. It was agreed that the children should receive £15,000 each as their cash share of the will.

Mary Birchall outlived her husband by over 20 years and after her death, Ribbleton Hall was rented to Nicholas Le Gendre Starkie who remained there for many years.

About 1926 it was sold to Mr. George Moorcroft, who converted the Hall into flats. During the Second World War it was requisitioned by the Government for billeting U.S. troops and after the War it was purchased by Preston Corporation. It was then demolished and the site used for the building of Moor Nook Primary School in Ribbleton Hall Drive.

Postscript on Mayor Birchall

The plight of Mary Birchall was noted in legal circles and no doubt her case played a significant part in the changing of the Inheritance Laws affecting wives.

The Attempted Murder of Samuel Horrocks M.P.

ON 4th April, 1823, Samuel Horrocks, Member of Parliament for Preston, received an anonymous letter bearing a Manchester postmark, at his Lark Hill residence. The letter was a threatening one and one that the co-founder of the Horrockses cotton empire would have done well to have taken very seriously.

Poor conditions in the cotton mills of the day and a general discontent had led the workers to unite in opposing the unscrupulous ways of the cotton masters.

The contents of the letter were as follows:

"Sir if you do not advance the wages of cotton spinners at least 20 per cent you may expect your life to be taken by a cotton spinner from Manchester. You was the cause of the falling of wages in Preson. Preston spinners are working more than 20 per cent under Manchester, and I understand that the spinners at Bolton and their masters are at difference about dropping the wages there. The masters offer them more than you give, but I hope they will be obliged to give them the same as they had before. There are many cotton masters deserve to lose their lives, but you are, it is said and I believe it is true, the worst of them all; therefore your life must go first, and the rest in rotation".

Samuel Horrocks 1766-1842, Mayor of Preston 1801-2, he survived attempted murder by Andrew Ryding in 1823.

It later turned out that the sender of the letter was a man by the name of Andrew Ryding. Ryding was a 22-year-old committee man of the Preston Union and regularly attended meetings at the Green Man public house in Lord Street.

For weeks after sending the letter Ryding remained in an agitated state and finally on 27th July, 1823, he decided to carry out his threat.

It was Sunday and as usual Samuel attended morning service at Preston Parish Church. On leaving the church he walked down Church Street with the intention of visiting his business partner, Thomas Miller, who lived in a large house in Golden Square. As he entered the gate which led to Mr. Miller's house, the Preston M.P. received a violent blow to the back of his head. He managed to turn round and saw a man brandishing a cleaver. The assailant struck again with three or four blows but with quick reflexes, Mr. Horrocks took the force of these blows on his arm.

The cleaver was then thrown or fell to the ground whereupon Mr. Horrocks grabbed hold of it and the attacker ran away. Ryding however, was apprehended by two onlookers who happened to be closeby.

On 18th August Andrew Ryding appeared at Lancaster Assizes

Preston Parish Church about 1828 and as it appeared when Samuel Horrocks attended church on Sunday, 27th July, 1823. After the morning service Samuel walked down Church Street towards the home of his business partner, but within minutes was confronted by a man brandishing a cleaver

charged with the attempted murder of Samuel Horrocks. The trial, which began at nine o'clock in the morning, lasted for over twelve hours and during the whole time the Court was crowded "almost to suffocation".

The trial revealed that the defendant had been the author of the threatening letter and in a long address to the jury the prisoner detailed the many reasons for this actions. He stated that Mr. Horrocks and Mr. Miller were the sole cause of the falling in wages in the cotton mills and the result of workers' strike action over a 10 per cent reduction in wages. Many of them had been unfairly imprisoned in the House of Correction, for striking without notice. His well delivered speech referred to his personal torment as he agonised over whether to attack Samuel Horrocks in a bid to bring to the public's attention the injustices of the cotton industry.

With the prisoner having admitted his actions the defence case evolved around his sanity. His lawyers claimed he had lost the sense of reason — necessary to know right from wrong — as such he could not be responsible for his actions.

At the end of a long day the jury retired to consider their verdict. While the jury was out the prisoner leaned upon the bar with his hands over his face. The jury returned within 10 minutes and brought with them a "Not Guilty" verdict "on the grounds of insanity". A pleased Andrew Ryding then addressed the jury and thanked them for patient attention and the fair and impartial trial he had received; but there was to be no walk to freedom for the assailant of Samuel Horrocks. Mr. Justice Bayley announced that, for the safety of the King's subject "a person in the condition of the prisoner must be detained in custody at the pleasure of His Majesty to prevent his doing further mischief".

Even though Ryding was detained in Lancaster Prison at the pleasure of His Majesty, Samuel Horrocks was still greatly concerned about Ryding's possible future release. To that end he wrote to Sir Robert Peel, Home Secretary, asking his reassurance on the matter.

He received the following reply:

> "My dear Sir, Andrew Ryding cannot be removed from the Castle at Lancaster without my authority, and I will take care that he shall not leave that place of custody without the greatest precaution. In the meantime, I shall be happy to receive any suggestions with respect to him which may appear to you worthy of my attention. I have the honour to be your obedient servant, Robert Peel."

Horrocks must have made a suggestion or suggestions because in November, 1823, he received a further letter from Sir Robert Peel:

> "My dear Sir, Supposing that Ryding were insane, the best place to send him to would no doubt be the criminal side of Bethlehem Hospital. But if he is not insane, that is not a fit place for his reception and the physicians would report upon his health and recommend his discharge. The only alternative is his confinement in a prison, for he cannot be transported. Now I doubt whether there is not less chance of his escape from Lancaster Castle than from any other prison in the kingdom . . . etc. I am dear Sir, very truly yours, Robert Peel".

Postscript on Samuel Horrocks

Samuel Horrocks remained as a Member of Parliament until 1826 and despite being a master cotton spinner and a shrewd businessman, was often criticised as incompetent in his role as an M.P. He very rarely spoke in the House of Commons and was known mockingly as "a silent member". Father of eight — seven daughters and one son, also named Samuel — he lived to the age of 76 and died at his Lark Hill, Preston home on 2nd March, 1842. He was buried in St. George's Churchyard, in the grave already occupied by his wife, Alice, who had predeceased him by some 38 years.

At the time of his death his only son, Sam, was the Guild Mayor of Preston.

The Slaying of Annie Ratcliffe

ON a Wednesday morning, early in August 1881, Ann Ratcliffe the 16-year-old daughter of the landlord of the Blue Bell Inn, Church Street, was excited. For this was to be the wedding day of herself and John Aspinall Simpson, aged 21, at St. Paul's Church, Preston.

She met her boyfriend outside the Blue Bell and together they walked up North Road to the Sir Walter Scott public house, which stood at the corner of North Road and Lord's Walk.

Once inside they were served with two glasses of lemonade by the landlady's daughter, they sat together on a seat near the window. Their attitude appeared to be very affectionate and they were left alone to consume their drinks. Some ten minutes later the landlady's daughter heard the sound of breaking glass and returned to the bar parlour to witness a most horrifying spectacle. Ann Ratcliffe came staggering towards her with a frightful gash in her throat. The unfortunate young woman was breathing her last and within seconds she was dead.

Simpson was sitting quietly on a bench nearby and appeared to show little concern for what he had done. When the girl asked him what he had done he made no reply. Lying on the floor beside him was

---

ALFRED RATCLIFFE,

BLUE BELL INN

114, CHURCH STREET,

PRESTON.

Home-brewed and other Ales, Choice Wines, and Superior Spirits.

A 19th century trade advertisement for the Blue Bell Inn, Church Street, which at the time was kept by Alfred Ratcliffe, father of Annie.

a razor which was smeared with blood. The landlady, Mrs. Ann Quigley, promptly sent a messenger to fetch the police, while two local men, who had arrived on the scene, kept Simpson in attendance.

Simpson was taken into police custody and under interrogation stated that he and the young woman had made an appointment to be married that very day. The unfortunate girl had been made pregnant by Simpson and was wearing her Sunday best in the belief that they were on their way to be married at St. Paul's Church. Her father had signed his consent to the wedding but had said he wanted no further part in it. Simpson further stated they were on their way to the church when they called at the Sir Walter Scott. On investigation, however, it appeared that no such notice of marriage had been given.

Throughout the day, the street in front of the public house was thronged with people anxious to get a glimpse of the room which had suddenly acquired such unbelievable notoriety. Public opinion was that the foul murder must have been premeditated and it was generally felt that Simpson could not have found a quieter street or a quieter public house to commit his foul deed. It was also later revealed that a couple of nights before the murder, Simpson, Miss Ratcliffe and another girl had been out on a pleasure boat on the River Ribble. Simpson had on that occasion attempted to overturn the boat but was unsuccessful in his intention. The girls being somewhat alarmed at Simpson's actions, demanded to be taken off the boat and he acceded to their wishes.

The couple had been keeping company for about two years and were deeply attached to each other according to reports. Nevertheless her father had been non-too-keen on the acquaintance and had tried every means to break off their friendship.

Simpson was a familiar figure on the streets of Preston He was an ostentatious dresser, who liked to display rings and other jewellery; occasionally he would also sport a smart walking stick. Having been born and brought up in Preston and having been employed in public offices in the town, he was one of the best known young men in the Borough. Unknown to his mother and his sisters, he managed to get clothes and whatever else he wanted by pledging her credit.

Miss Ratcliffe was brought to Preston from Darwen in 1872. She was educated at the national schools of the parishes of St. Paul's and St. James. On leaving school, she assisted her father in the Blue Bell Inn. Less than two years before her untimely end, her mother had died, an occurrence which caused her deep distress.

At the subsequent trial, John Aspinall Simpson made no attempt to defend himself. He neither confessed nor denied the charge. With such overwhelming evidence against him he was duly found guilty of the murder and sentenced to death.

On Saturday, November 26th, 1881, he received a final visit from his younger sister, Miss Lizzie Simpson, who conveyed a message of forgiveness from the dead girl's father who had declined Simpson's invitation for him to visit the prison. It was a painful interview for the sister of the murderer, who stated afterwards that her brother was quite resigned to his fate.

The following Tuesday morning a crowd of several hundred gathered outside of Strangeways Prison, Manchester, to await the hoisting of the black flag to indicate that sentence had been carried out. At about a quarter-to-eight, executioner Marwood entered the condemned cell to make preparations for the carrying out of his task. As the procession of death made its way, the condemned man walked unaided to the scaffold. The skilful Marwood had already prepared a drop of between eight and nine feet to suit a man of below average height and weight

Picture reproduced by kind permission of the Lancashire Evening Post

After John Simpson was executed this memorial card was produced which showed a picture of Annie Ratcliffe together with her lover and killer, John Simpson. Before his execution his only request was that a photograph of himself and Annie be buried with him.

and death was almost instantaneous.

The crowd of sightseers began to disperse once the black flag had been hoisted, although a few loitered around the prison entrance, in the hope of catching a glimpse of the executioner.

Many memorial cards were printed in memory of Annie Ratcliffe and on the bottom of the card the following verse was inscribed.

That lovely morn I fully hoped I should become a wife
And had no fear that one so dear would take away my life
But death doth come in many forms — though painful was my lot
I pray for those I've left behind, and say,"Forget me not".

The Disappearance of Anthony Henry

MONDAY, 3rd September, 1883, was a wet day in Preston and as a result a group of harvest workers were rained off. To while-away their time they gathered in the Bakers Arms public house in Lawson Street, opposite the old gas works, and played a few games of cards. Among the group were 21-year-old Paddy McGinty and fellow Irishman Anthony Henry. Whilst playing a game called "twenty-fives" the two men started to quarrel. Following the intercession of their mates, the pair shook hands and all was once again peaceful.

After a little more time had elapsed Anthony Henry left the beer-house and returned to his lodgings at 13 Atkinson Street, there he took a knife off the table in the back kitchen and knelt down to sharpen it on the doorstep. He then placed the knife in his trouser pocket, left his lodgings and made his way back to the Bakers Arms. Somehow word got back to McGinty that Henry was after him, armed with a knife. McGinty immediately left the public house and entered Lawson Street where the two Irishmen met. Henry, brandishing the weapon, moved towards McGinty and struck him a blow on the left hand side of the head. As soon as the deed was done Henry turned and ran away from the scene.

Blood was pouring from McGinty's head wound and with the aid of a few of the fellows from the beerhouse, was taken to a nearby druggist's shop. Medical assistance was soon on hand and McGinty was taken to the Infirmary. The incident had taken place at around three o'clock in the afternoon and by six o'clock he had died — without gaining consciousness.

At the Inquest, the afternoon's happenings were revealed and among the witnesses was Patrick Henry, younger brother of the missing Anthony Henry. He stated that his brother had been in the country about four years and that, like himself, was working on harvesting. He related how he had been in the Bakers Arms prior to the incident and that when he entered the street he had seen a crowd of people around McGinty and his brother stood further down the road. When he went towards his brother, he turned and ran away.

In his summing up, the Coroner said there was some evidence to implicate Anthony Henry for the death of Paddy McGinty, but his whereabouts was a mystery. That he was the person who made the attack on the deceased, there was little doubt. There seemed no other conclusion than that when he had left the public house he was intent on returning to avenge the quarrel, which seemed to have arisen from a slight cause.

The jury returned to consider the evidence and after an absence of ten minutes they returned. The foreman stood up and announced: "The unanimous verdict of the jury is one of Wilful Murder".

The search for Anthony Henry was intensified and gradually his getaway was pieced-together. He was believed to have run up Walker Street and past the Craven Heifer public house at the corner of North Road and Park Road. His path was traced to the St. Ignatius Girls' School yard off Meadow Street and then he was said to have climbed a wall into Sedgwick Street. In that street he approached a coachman to give him a lift, as the police were then after him. The coachman however refused and that was the last that was seen of the fugitive.

Part of St. Ignatius school and yard off Meadow Street in the early years of this century. It was through here that Anthony Henry passed in September 1883, to make good his escape from justice for murder. He was never seen of or heard of again.

A couple of days later the caretaker from the school found a blood-stained carving knife in the school ashpit. Examination of this showed that it was the murder weapon.

Baffled by the whereabouts of the accused, the police offered a £100 reward to anyone, except a police officer, giving information which would lead to his arrest. To aid would-be informers, a description of Anthony Henry was circulated and it included the following: "He had prominent teeth and it is with great difficulty that he covers them". Alas nothing further was ever heard of the Irish harvest worker and to this day the crime still ranks as one of the great mystery's of Preston's past.

The Shocking Murder
of a Sweetheart

"SHOCKING Murder of a Sweetheart in Preston", read the *Preston Chronicle* headline on a Saturday in mid-May, 1887. The victim was a young Irish woman named Annie Kelly who came from County Mayo in Western Ireland. She had been a laundry maid at the Bull Hotel in Church Street. The scene of the terrible tragedy was a coffee room at the Clarendon Temperance Hotel on Fishergate Hill. Her assailant was her lover, 23-year-old Alfred Sowrey, of 14 Stanleyfield Road, Preston, who assisted his brother in a pawnbroker's business in Queen Street.

One Wednesday afternoon, the couple entered the hotel at about a quarter to three and asked if they could have a meal. Met by the proprietor's daughter they were told they were too late for a main meal but that chops and potatoes were still available.

The young assistant then showed them into the coffee room while the food was being prepared. They had not been on the premises for more than five minutes when the sound of a revolver was heard. Returning to the coffee room, the assistant saw Annie Kelly slumped in a chair with a bullet wound in her temple. Alfred Sowrey was standing close-by with the revolver pointed at his own head. Four times he pulled the trigger but each time the cartridge failed to explode.

By now the proprietor, Mrs. Whitlock, was on the scene and assistance was soon on hand from the County Constabulary headquarters on Fishergate Hill. When Inspector Durham arrived, Sowrey was sat in a chair with the gun in his hand. At the Inspector's request he placed the gun on the table and when asked: "Who did this", he replied: "I did, and that is the revolver I did it with; I would have shot myself only the revolver misfired; I am sorry I did not do myself".

A doctor had been called to the girl's aid but when he arrived she was barely alive. The bullet wound was just beside the right eye and blood was flowing from the wound. She was beyond all medical help and life quickly ebbed away. Her head was inclined to the left shoulder and it appeared that Sowrey had forced her head on one side while he fired the shot.

Once in custody, Sowrey elaborated on his story by saying that his victim was "Annie Kelly, laundress of the Bull Hotel, but she got

The historic Bull Head Hotel in Church Street, where Annie Kelly worked as a laundry maid and where she made her fatal plans to emigrate with her sweetheart, Alfred Sowrey.

discharged from her situation through me on Monday. I am a single man, but should have been married today".

Gradually the story behind the terrible tragedy was pieced together. The couple had seemingly made plans to emigrate to the United States of America together, but the girl had insisted that she would only leave on condition that they were first married before they embarked on their journey.

On the Monday before her death, Miss Kelly had been dismissed from her job at the Bull Hotel, for failing to return the previous evening, and on the Monday night she had stayed with friends in Christ Church Place. On the Tuesday morning, Sowrey had purchased the 'British Bulldog' revolver, for 12s. 6d. (62^1/2 new pence), which he used for the killing.

The conclusion drawn was that Sowrey had been reluctant to marry the 19-year-old laundry maid and as a result she had been unwilling to accompany him and had refused to board the train from Preston Station. There seemed to be a certain amount of premeditation in his actions due to the fact that he had purchased the gun, although no real motive for the crime came to light.

For Annie Kelly, there was great public sympathy and when it was known that her parents were too poor to leave Ireland for her funeral, an organised collection was made in the town. Almost 2,000 people followed the funeral cortege to the graveside and a memorial cross was erected over her last resting place at Preston Cemetery. The inscription on the celtic cross stated: "This monument was erected by sympathetic contributors who believed she died in defence of her virtue".

By the time Sowrey appeared at Lancaster Assizes charged with her murder, he had changed his plea to "Not Guilty". However the jury had no hesitation in finding him guilty and he was duly sentenced to hang. His trial took place in July, 1887. Three weeks later he was despatched from this life. While awaiting his fate he asked the prison chaplain to send Annie Kelly's parents a letter of contrition on his behalf.

In Preston Cemetery stands this magnificent Celtic Cross funded by an organised collection in the town to mark the last resting place of laundry maid Annie Kelly.

The Trial of Doctor Monk

ON Thursday, 18th February, 1858, long before the doors were opened, there was a large crowd of people outside the doors of Lancaster Assizes. Among the crowd were a large number of visitors from Preston, all anxious to be present at the trial of Dr. Thomas Monk, former Mayor of Preston, for forging the will of Edward Turner and uttering the same, knowing it to be forged.

Edward Turner had died on 25th February, 1857. At the time of Turner's death. Dr. Thomas Monk, the senior Alderman of the borough, had been attending to the medical needs of the 70-year- old reedmaker, who resided in St. Pauls Road, Preston.

The doors were opened at 10 o'clock, immediately followed by a great rush of people into the Crown Court. The assembly included many personal friends of Dr. Monk. As well as the normal train service bringing visitors from Preston, a special train had additionally been laid on to enable everyone interested, the opportunity to be present at the trial.

The accused man was a well known figure in the town — having begun in medical practice, in Preston, in 1820. Thomas Monk had been born at Bispham, near Ormskirk, and had served a medical apprenticeship in Preston's apothecary hall. Following the Municipal Reform Act of 1835, he was elected a Councillor for Trinity Ward and in November 1837 became an Alderman. In 1851 his service was recognised when he was selected as Mayor of the Borough, Among his many mayoral duties he presided at the opening of the new Fire Station in Tithebarn Street and at the unveiling of the statue of Robert Peel in Winckley Square.

When Monk appeared in the dock, the prisoner seemed weak and somewhat disconcerted by the gaze of the immense assemblage, among whom he recognised many familiar faces. After the Clerk of the Court had read out the indictment the prisoner replied in a loud tone of voice — "Not Guilty".

The day's proceedings revealed that the day after Turner's death, Monk had called at the Lancaster Banking Co. in Preston to draw out money from the dead man's account, which he claimed was needed to pay wages to the deceased man's three employees.

Monk claimed that he was the principal creditor and he signed on oath that the estate was under £100. He was informed that letters of administration would have to be obtained before any further action could be taken about the money.

A few days later he returned to the bank and claimed he had found Turner's will which had left a small sum to a female relative — 3 shillings per week to the housekeeper and the rest, about £50, to himself. Inspection of the will aroused suspicion and enquiries took place into its authenticity.

One of the witnesses called was a Mrs. Pike, the wife of a hairdresser from Fishergate. She revealed how Dr. Monk had persuaded her to innocently copy the will for him, with the instructions to make the writing large like a mans. She also admitted writing the name of one of the two witnesses.

The document was dated 14th February, 1857. She admitted writing it on 28th February, 1857, some three days after Turner's death. She also stated that when she took it to Dr. Monk it did not have the signatures of Edward Turner or the witness, Joseph Wilkinson on it, but only the name of one witness, James Holden, whose name she had written.

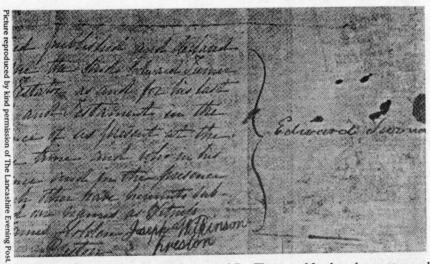

A copy of the forged will which caused Dr. Thomas Monk to be sentenced to "Penal Servitude for Life". He added the names 'Edward Turner' and 'Joseph Wilkinson'.

The housekeeper for Dr. Monk also gave evidence and disclosed that following her master's death, the accused had taken away his deed box and arranged the funeral himself. she also claimed that he took possession of Turner's silver teaspoons and a picture of Robert Peel, and that far from being a close friend of the deceased the accused had only attended her master during the final fortnight of his illness.

The jury also heard how, following the investigation into the validity of the will, there were persistent rumours that Monk had actually poisoned Turner. At this, exhumation took place. A coroner's inquest was held on the body and at one stage a charge of murdering Edward Turner was actually brought against the accused, although following further investigation the charge was dropped.

Monk's counsel claimed that he had not acted like a guilty man and that if he had been guilty, of even the forging of the will, he had had ample time to flee, rather than continue his medical practice in the town prior to his eventual arrest.

By late afternoon all the evidence had been presented and the judge briefly summed up, emphasising the credibility of a number of the prosecution witnesses.

The jury then huddled together in the box with their backs to the accused. After five minutes consultation, the foreman delivered a "Guilty" verdict on their behalf.

With the prisoner standing, the judge addressed him saying he had been convicted on the clearest of evidence, and that for a man of his public standing the offence was a disgraceful one. He went on to remark about the unethical way in which he, a medical man, had taken advantage of the position of confidence in which he was trusted. Finally saying that for the sake of the public, an example needed to be made of him and therefore the sentence of the Court is that "You be subjected to Penal Servitude for life".

His career and future in ruins, the disgraced surgeon heaved a deep sigh and descended the steps of the dock out of sight of the now silent court room.

One week later a statement appeared in the 'Preston Chronicle following an interview with Monk in Lancaster Castle. In it he attempted to expose what he called the mis- statements of witnesses at the trial but his lengthy narrative did little to convince people of his innocence.

Within three weeks Monk was on his way to London's Millbank Penitentiary. As the carriage passed through Preston Railway Station,

Following Dr. Thomas Monk's conviction of forgery his name was removed both from the base of Peel's statue (above) in Winckley Square which he unveiled and also from the old fire station (right) in Tithebarn Street which he opened during his mayoral year of 1851-2. One of the few surviving records of Dr. Monk's mayoralty is permanently captured in Hewitson's 'History of Preston' (below).

1847 Thos. Birchall.
1848 Richard Pedder.
1849 James German.
1850 John Catterall.
→ 1851 Thomas Monk.
1852 Peter Catterall.
1853 Thomas Walmsley.
1854 Wm. Humber.
1855 Rich. Threlfall.

the blinds were drawn and no one was allowed to see him. Shortly afterwards Preston Corporation removed the name of the disgraced Alderman from the Peel Statue and also from the new Fire Station in Tithebarn Street.

Postscript on Dr. Thomas Monk

When convicted, Monk was 61-years-old. His 'Particulars of Convict' details described him as 5ft. 9ins. tall, of pale complexion with grey hair and no distinguishing marks. He served ten years hard labour before being released from Woking prison on 26th March, 1868, to return to Preston where he once more resumed medical practice.

Surprisingly he became well liked among his patients and was eventually appointed physician to the Preston Oddfellows. His sentence was finally revoked in 1880, when he was 80 years of age.

After his return to Preston he had lived for a time at 49 Frenchwood Street and in his later years at 147 Church Street, above a chemist's shop. It was there that he died after a six month's illness at the great age of 89 in 1888.

When details of his will were revealed, his estate was valued at £9,000. He left £4,000 of this to his wife Sophia and the remainder was shared between his godchild and a few friends.

Drownings at Chain Pit

ON the first Saturday in November, 1861, the residents of Preston were startled by the appearance, on hoardings, of posters headed "Murder" and stating that the dead body of a male child, "to all appearance twelve months old, very fat, and in a healthy condition, sandy haired and full-faced", had, that afternoon, "been found in a pit near a footpath in the township of Ashton, near Preston".

The discovery had been made by two young men walking along a nearby footpath who had observed something floating on the water of a large pit known as the Chain Pit. Filled with terror at the discovery of the child's body the young men fled to Preston and told the story of their discovery to some of their acquaintances.

Once the police got notice of the tale some officers were immediately despatched to the pit and the child taken out of the water to be conveyed to a stable adjoining the Plough Inn. The child was clothed

The Plough Hotel, the adjacent stable of which was used for the inquest on the child found drowned in Chain Pit.

in neatly made garments; all that was missing was possibly its cap or hat. It was felt that this may have sunk and could help in identification and so it was decided to search the pit the following morning.

For that purpose a local wheelwright made some grappling irons to drag the pit which was about 20 yards in diameter and about 5 yards deep in the centre. The police constables started their search and very soon the irons struck against something massive at the bottom of the centre of the pit. Within a few minutes the full horror of the situation became apparent, when they pulled out the body of a woman in her early twenties, who, they immediately assumed, was the mother of the child. Close examination suggested that the woman had been in the pit for about a week and later investigations showed this to be correct. A couple of people who lived in the vicinity of the pit recalled how a few days before they had seen the woman sitting by the water with a child in her arms. She had been there when they set out on their errand and was still there when they returned along the nearby footpath. They had seen nothing to make them suspicious and nothing to suspect foul play.

The water at the edge of the pit was shallow and its bed was of gradual descent and so it was determined that she must have deliberately gone out of her way to get to the deep water in the centre. The police also considered the possibility that perhaps the child had slipped into the water and that the mother had attempted a rescue. This idea was ruled out as the pit was so shallow for a considerable distance, that such a rescue would have been a simple task. The final conclusion they came to was that she had, in a state of desperation, owing to poverty and shame, first thrown her child into the water and then drowned herself.

While all the activity was going on at the pit, the posters in Preston were receiving much attention. Attracted by a crowd of people intently engaged in reading a poster in Lune Street, a Mrs. Preston from 298 North Road, crossed over to catch a glimpse of the news. On reading the details of the baby boy's tragic end, she became horrified as she realised that the description of the child's pinafore exactly tallied with one which she had made. She hastened home and revealed the news to her husband and son, who immediately accompanied her to Ashton.

Her husband, Stephen Preston, asked to be admitted to view the child's body and when shown the mother and son side by side he cried out: "That's Ann Wright and her little Charlie". He could hardly restrain his sorrow and it was only with some difficulty that the officer in charge elicited from him that she was a single woman and the daughter of John Wright, who kept the ferry boat over the Ribble at Warton Banks, between Freckleton and Lytham.

Following this identification, details of the young woman's distressing past was revealed. Desertion by her heartless seducer, combined with an unhappy train of trials through which it had been her fate to pass since the birth of her child, had no doubt led her to carry out the dreadful deed.

It transpired that Mrs. Preston had been like a "sister of mercy" to the unfortunate girl and it was at the Preston's home that she had given birth to her child, 14 months before. After the confinement, Mrs. Preston nursed the girl back to health and looked after the child until Ann Wright got a situation in a Blackpool boarding house.

Mrs. Preston was anxious that the child should have a permanent home and wrote to the girl's father at Warton. There was no assistance forthcoming from the man and unfortunately, after caring for the child for eight months, the Preston family were unable to continue their benevolence due to their changed circumstances.

For a few months the distraught girl went from situation to situation but still struggled to obtain a livelihood. In an attempt to secure her child's future, she tried at the Blackpool petty sessions to affiliate the child, alleging that his father was a young man named Kenyon, a blacksmith from Wigan. She failed however with Kenyon, after he asserted that he had seen her coquetting with other men.

A week before her sad end she appeared at Mrs. Preston's home to show her the healthy looking baby. The ever-helpful Mrs. Preston tried to help her obtain a position as a household domestic but she was unsuccessful. The girl then asked Mrs. Preston if once again she would take her son into her safe-keeping, but although she herself was willing, she had to refuse because of her husband's unwillingness.

Ann Wright then talked of going to Liverpool or some other place she did not know in the hope of bettering her situation. A concerned Mrs. Preston suggested that the child may be better off taken to the workhouse but the young mother rebuffed the suggestion.

After spending the night at the Preston household, Ann Wright left saying she was going to Lune Street. As she left she said to Mrs. Preston: "The next thing you hear of me, it will be something very strange". Sadly those words were to be true as the girl's sad end was revealed.

At the inquest consideration was given of the girl's unfortunate existence and under the Coroner's direction recorded was an open verdict of "Found Drowned". It was felt there was not sufficient evidence to prove that she intended self destruction or that she intended to destroy her child.

Tragedy at Fulwood Barracks

IN 1861, Patrick McCaffery was a 19-year-old private serving at Fulwood Barracks under the command of Colonel Crofton and his adjutant Captain Hanham, a strict disciplinarian. On several occasions McCaffery had been punished by his superior officers for various offences and had been sentenced to 'pack drill' and cell confinement.

He was described by his colleagues as a loner, rather quiet and studious and one who would frequently sit up in bed for hours reading books. He formed no friendships and did not seek the companionship of his fellow soldiers. When affected with any of the larks that soldiers in barracks are prone to, he would laugh sarcastically, leading them to suppose that he intended reprisals.

On Friday, 13th September, 1861, he was assigned to the duty of 'picket sentry' by Captain Hanham. Part of his duty was to keep the footway adjoining the officers quarters clear of children. Some of the window panes had previously been broken and the officers themselves had been made to pay for their replacement. Private Mcaffery was neglectful in

A soldier in the uniform of the 1860s.

Picture by kind permission of the Lancashire Evening Post.

his duty and when Captain Hanham saw three children in the vicinity of the officers quarters he ordered Private McCaffery to pursue them and find out the names of their parents.

Somewhat reluctantly, McCaffery went after the children but when he returned he had only details of one of the children. The Captain was rather displeased with McCaffery's efforts and ordered him to be confined in the guard house overnight. The following morning he was taken before the commanding officer and was ordered to be confined to Barracks for fourteen days — a punishment that included an extra four hours drill each day. After being taken to the guard house, to be shown to the sergeant of the guard so that he might know him and prevent him leaving the barracks, he was once again placed at liberty within the barracks.

As mid-day approached Colonel Crofton and Captain Hanham were together walking briskly across the barracks square. When they came into the view of Private McCaffery, who was kneeling outside the door of eastern block with a rifle at his shoulder, he calmly took aim at the officers and fired the rifle. The bullet struck the Colonel in the right lung and passed through his body into the left arm of the Captain and finally came to rest in his chest. Private McCaffery then calmly handed his rifle to a corporal and gave himself up.

Both officers were immediately given medical assistance but the bullet had caused much damage. Colonel Crofton eventually died due to an internal hemorrhage in the substance of the lung and Captain Hanham, who was in much pain, died the following day, despite removal of the deeply embedded bullet.

The terrible tragedy startled the whole country by its enormity with accompanying deep feelings of horror at the deed. The removal of the bodies of the two officers from the Barracks to the railway station for transit to their homes for burial, created much interest. Great numbers of people congregated on the roads leading to the Barracks. Business establishments on the route closed, as the gun carriages bearing union-jack draped coffins made their way to the station.

When questioned about the shootings, Private McCaffery said that he had not intended to shoot the Colonel, but was aiming to wound the Captain. Whatever his intentions he had succeeded in committing the most terrible of crimes. Within days he was removed from Preston Gaol to Kirkdale Gaol, to await trial at Liverpool Assizes. He was moved early in the morning so that public attention could be avoided, as there were fears that an indignant public may subject him to summary punishment.

When the trial took place the young soldier was found guilty of the double murder and was sentenced to hang. His public execution took place outside Kirkdale Prison, Liverpool.

When I was just sixteen years of age,
To the British Army I did engage;
I left my home with good intent
To join the forty-second regiment.

To Fulwood Barracks I did go,
To serve my time in that depot.
From troubles then I was never free:
My captain took a great dislike to me.

When posted on duty at the barrack gate,
Some soldiers' children came to play;
From the officers' mess my captain came
And ordered me to take their parents' name.

I took one name instead of three;
'Neglect of duty' they did charge me:
Ten days' C.B. and the loss of pay,
That's what it cost me for those children's play.

With a loaded rifle I did swear
I'd shoot my captain on the barrack square;
I aimed my rifle and fired to kill,
And hit my colonel against my will.

At the Liverpool Assizes my trial I stood;
The jury they all banged on wood.
The judge he said, 'McCaffery,
Prepare yourself for the gallows tree'.

Well, I've no mother to break her heart;
I've no father to take my part.
I have only one friend, and a girl is she;
She'd lay her life down for McCaffery.

Come all you young officers of the present day,
Just treat your men with civility,
For if you don't, there's sure to be
Another hard case like McCaffery.

The melancholy story of Private Patrick McCaffery was composed to music and for half a pence each, printed ballad sheets were sold nationwide.

Murder in Bleasdale Street

DURING Whitsuntide, 1875, Mark Fiddler carried out a threat often previously uttered, of breaking up the home he shared with his wife of four years, Dorothy Fiddler. The little furniture they had was sold and the wife was left to go where she pleased. Mark Fiddler, a 24-year-old cotton spinner, described as a man of dissolute habits and of a passionate and jealous nature, soon squandered the proceeds of the sale in local ale houses. His wife, meanwhile, had taken- up lodgings at the house of William Green, a fish dealer, on Ribbleton Lane, at the corner of Bleasdale Street.

Mark Fiddler, his money now gone, left the town for a short period, but soon returned to pay frequent visits to his estranged wife. He detained her often in the streets until a late hour and received money from her for provisions and tobacco.

He managed to obtain lodgings at 3 St. Mary's Gate, with a couple of military acquaintances. At around half past six on Tuesday night, 8th June, 1875, he left his lodgings with a cut-throat razor in his possession, to pay one of his regular visits to his wife. Later that evening he was seen in her company along Bleasdale Street and around St. Luke's Church, by a number of people, between 8 o'clock and 11 o'clock. As the evening drew to a close the couple headed back to Dorothy Fiddler's lodgings and stood outside the side door in Bleasdale Street. Soon a scuffle was heard outside the premises and within seconds Dorothy Fiddler staggered through the door with blood pouring from her throat. Within ten minutes she was dead.

Immediately after the scuffle, Mark Fiddler was seen to run off down Bleasdale Street. At once a search was made for him by the police and at half past one in the morning, he was found swimming fully clothed in the lodge of Messrs. Lancaster and Isherwoods Mill at the bottom of Bleasdale Street. When he reached the middle of the Lodge he raised his right hand to his throat and appeared to cut himself with a razor. He sank twice but came to the surface and eventually swam to the side. He was immediately apprehended and it was noticed that he had a two inch long wound on the left hand side of his neck. He was given some brandy and taken to the Infirmary.

An hour later he seemed to recover from his ordeal and was charged with the wilful murder of his wife, in response to which he made no reply.

He appeared on the charge at Lancaster Assizes on 27th June. It was rumoured before the trial, that an attempt would be made to mitigate the severity of the Law, by including evidence of his wife's unchastity. In the event, his counsel did not assail the character of the murdered woman but chose instead to suggest that the diabolical deed was the act of a madman. They claimed that it was impossible to conceive that a sane person, impelled by no inciting motive whatever, could be guilty of such a brutal murder.

The Judge, Mr. Justice Archibald, summed up totally against this first theory and the jury had little difficulty in reaching a verdict of "Guilty" of the crime described as most foul and atrocious. The judge duly passed the sentence of death.

Following the sentencing, no attempt was made to procure a remittance of the death penalty, as it was felt it would be a hopeless exercise. From the moment he was apprehended, he seemed resigned to his fate and never claimed it was not merited.

On Monday, 16th August, 1875, as the citizens of Lancaster were arousing themselves for the business of their daily lives, Mark Fiddler and William McCullough (guilty of a murder at Barrow), were preparing for their fate. The executions were timed for eight o'clock at Lancaster Castle and executioner, William Marwood, had been preparing the gallows from early morning.

Both the murderers had slept until around four o'clock and then been offered breakfast. McCullough ate a good breakfast but Fiddler declined any food. With the time approaching six o'clock, the two men dressed and waited in the company of the chaplain for the fateful hour.

As soon as the last echo of the clock struck eight, the voice of the chaplain was heard pronouncing the words from the burial service: "I am the resurrection and the life", as the procession to the scaffold began. The chaplain led the way dressed in his white robes of office, then came two jailers, followed by the criminals. The deputy governor, the executioner and two more jailers brought up the rear. Fiddler and McCullough ascended the steps to the gallows attired in the clothes they wore at the time of their apprehension. The executioner, who wore a black frock coat, assisted them to their respective positions, where both men immediately dropped onto their knees. With heads raised upwards both cried out: "Lord, receive my spirit". After a couple of minutes the men stood up and the executioner placed white hoods over their faces. Fiddler seemed to be about 5ft. 3ins. tall, of stout build with a short thick neck, while McCullough appeared to be about 5ft. 9ins. tall and of a much thinner build. The executioner, who was a quiet reserved man in his mid fifties, set about fixing the noose and placing the prisoners in their proper positions.

Marwood, the executioner, then descended the steps and took his place on a small stool at the end of the scaffold. After a brief period of suspense, the drop fell. A dull thud and a little resonance from the sinking timbers were the only sounds that accompanied the awful event. Fiddler, whose knees had trembled while standing in fearful anticipation, was seen to jolt violently upwards about ten times after falling with a convulsive motion of the shoulders. His body finally quivered for a few moments before signs of life ceased. McCullough, on the other hand, who was firm and unmoved on the scaffold, died after a feeble movement of his frame had been observed.

The doorway from the Chapel Room into the Drop Room in Lancaster Castle, through which the chaplain led Mark Fiddler and William McCullough to executioner Marwood.

The executions were witnessed by a small group of spectators, made up of prison officials and members of the Press. In all, seven minutes elapsed from the appearance of the prisoners to the time that their bodies showed no sign of life. A black flag was then hoisted over the Gateway Tower to inform the neighbourhood that the extreme sentence of the Law had been carried out.

Following the inquest into their executions, the bodies of the two men were interred in the corner of the Castle precincts.

The Slaying of a Church Street Butcher

THE day started in the usual manner in the Church Street, butchers shop of Albert Dewhurst. It was 18th April, 1906. At around 6.30 a.m. Mr. Dewhurst's assistant, Samuel Massey, who lived in nearby Meadow Street, arrived and the two men set about their work in preparation for the day's trading.

A few minutes later, Alice Dewhurst, the butcher's wife, came downstairs. According to Mr. Massey, she looked a little upset but he put it down to "pains in the head", which he knew had, in the past, affected her health.

After a cup of tea, Mrs. Dewhurst too joined the men at work in the shop. Mr. Dewhurst cut up the meat while Mrs. Dewhurst made out the entries in the order book.

The orders prepared, Mr. Dewhurst indicated that he would now make his usual morning visit to the cattle market. His wife replied: "All right, I can manage".

The atmosphere in the shop seemed quite relaxed and friendly as the butcher left to catch a tram. He returned to the shop a little time later, having realised that he had missed his intended tram.

On entering the premises his assistant remarked that he would have to catch a later tram, as Mr. Dewhurst was passing him on his way into the kitchen at the rear of the shop.

As the 42-year-old butcher entered the kitchen he was struck with terror. His wife, without warning and without uttering a word was rushing towards him brandishing a butcher's knife in each hand. She lunged at him with each knife in the region of his heart and also his shoulder. The unfortunate man fell to the floor in the doorway between the shop and kitchen clasping his hand to his heart and moaning. The two knives still in her hands, Alice Dewhurst, then made off upstairs, leaving the shocked assistant to tend the fatally injured butcher.

It was close to 7.30 a.m., when the assistant raised the alarm. On duty in the neighbourhood was a P.C. Jones. When the constable arrived on the scene, he found the butcher lying on his back and bleeding profusely from the injuries inflicted. He immediately summoned a doctor, then commenced the brave task of trying to locate the deranged woman with two knives. On reaching the first floor landing he found a bedroom door locked and without more ado, burst it open. A most horrifying sight met him. Alice Dewhurst was standing over the bed, the two knives held high and poised to strike the couple's 10-year-old daughter.

An idyllic picture of the Dewhurst family which to all appearances was a happy and contented one. Married for 11 years the Dewhursts had three children but only one survived early childhood.

Without thought for personal safety, the constable, together with a colleague who by now had arrived on the scene, rushed at the woman and were able to wrest the knives from her hands. Alice Dewhurst appeared demented but was eventually overpowered and taken to the police station.

Nothing could be done for her husband, Albert Dewhurst, shortly after his wife had been taken away from the premises, he died.

When later charged with the offence Mrs. Dewhurst seemed completely oblivious to the severity of her actions and the position in which she now found herself, and replied: "He's not dead is he?"

The tragedy shocked the community, as the couple were regarded as a happy and contented pair. Mr. Dewhurst had been a member of the Preston Burchers Association from its inception and had also been a committee member for 10 years. He was recognised as a devout Catholic who was a regular attender at the nearby St. Augustine's Church. A family friend revealed that only a few days before, they had been together on an outing to Blackpool and there had been no indication of any problems between them although the wife had been ailing for some time.

There seemed little doubt that without the prompt action of the two police constables the tragedy would have been even greater by the intended murder of Mary Dewhurst, the couple' daughter.

On 7th May, 1906, Margaret Alice Dewhurst, aged 38, appeared at Liverpool Assizes, accused of killing her husband. It was generally accepted that nothing other than a fit of madness could have brought about the tragedy. Medical evidence was produced to show that she was in no fit state to plead. She had obviously been affected by the tragedy and showed little sign of the required sanity to conduct her defence. In the circumstances the judge descided he had no alternative but to order her to be detained during His Majesty's Pleasure.

Little could the unfortunate butcher have known what lay in wait for him when he returned home after missing the early morning tram.

Wife Killing at the Grapes Hotel

IN the year 1913, John Jones, a former regular soldier, married a woman of low repute by the name of Mary. From the start Jones was determined to reform his new wife and to that end set up home in Back Millbank, off Church Street, Preston.

About a year after their marriage, Mary Jones decided to resume her previous low life by leaving her husband to live with a woman friend who was a prostitute.

On Saturday, July 18th, 1914, John Jones had been drinking in the town centre, when he heard that his wife and her friend were in the Grapes Hotel (now the Bears Paw), in Church Street. He arrived there about 8 p.m. with the intention of trying to persuade his wife to return

The Grapes Hotel (now the Bears Paw) was the scene of the killing of Mary Jones, a woman of low repute, by her husband.

home.

He accused his wife's companion of leading her astray and inevitably a quarrel developed, resulting in him getting hold of the woman's throat. His wife then intervened and Jones said to her: "I will do for you then".

He then put his arm round his wife's neck drew a razor from his pocket and ran it across her throat. Releasing her, he then proceeded to pull the razor twice across his own throat. Jones then staggered towards his dying wife, under the gaze of the pub's customers, and asked: "Can I kiss her before she dies?"

A local constable was on the scene within minutes where he witnessed Mary Jones sitting on a form with blood pouring from a large wound in her throat and in a dying condition. John Jones was seated on the floor with his back to his wife and he too was bleeding from the throat.

The constable immediately rendered first aid but could do little for the woman, who died within a few minutes. In an attempt to stem the flow of blood from Jones's wound he tied a handerchief around his throat.

Jones was then rushed to Preston Royal Infirmary, where he eventually recovered. At the Infirmary he volunteered a statement which read: "I married her off the streets. I have done it and I think its for the best. After I had cut her throat, the razor would not cut mine. I intended us both to die together, if it was only to save her from further disgrace

Preston Infirmary early this century and where in July 1914, John Jones was rushed with a handkerchief around his neck to stem the flow of blood.

by going back on the streets".

The subsequent inquest returned a verdict of "Wilful Murder" under provocation and Jones was detained to await trial at the next Lancaster Assizes.

Towards the end of October, 1914, he stood before Judge Sankey and the Grand Jury of the Autumn Assizes.

The general picture was that the 32-year-old Jones was a decent man who had married a prostitute. His attempt to reform her had failed and he could not induce her to leave her former occupation.

One of the witnesses called was a police sergeant and he related an incident the week-end before the killing. On that particular evening, Jones had pointed out his wife to the police officer and asked him to make his wife leave a soldier with whom she was linking arms in the street. Jones and the sergeant had walked behind the deceased and her companion, and several times she had turned round and jeered at her husband. Her taunts and general attitude towards him were said to amount to provocation of the greatest kind.

The facts indicated that Jones had been drinking on the night of the killing and he had, according to acquaintances, uttered threats to harm his wife. The defence counsel, while not using drunkenness as an excuse, asked the jury to consider the befuddled condition of the prisoner at the time of the crime.

When Mr. Justice Sankey summed up he said that although drunkenness was not an excuse, it did sometimes alter the nature of the crime.

The jury then retired to consider their deliberations, taking into account his previous good character and his wife's poor reputation. They returned to find him "Not Guilty of Murder", but guilty of "Manslaughter". Whereupon His Lordship pronounced a sentence of Ten Years Penal Servitude.

The Sad End of Philip Samuel Park

ONE Sunday afternoon in August, 1922, a man was found shot through the head in the River Thames near Windsor. He was identified as Mr. Philip Samuel Park, aged 57, a former Mayor of Preston and Justice of the Peace for the town.

Mrs Philip Park
Mayoress of Preston

Councillor Philip Samuel Park
Mayor of Preston

News of the bizarre end to the life of Mr. Park surprised the people of Preston, who had been well served by Councillor Philip Park and by his father and grandfather before him. His grandfather, had himself been Mayor of Preston, in 1862-63, while his father had been a Borough Alderman and a Justice of the Peace for the County of Lancaster.

Philip Park's municipal career began in November, 1893, when he became a representative of the Maudland Ward. Just two years later, still aged only 30, he became Mayor of the Borough and was assisted in his duties by his second wife, Sarah Ellen Park, who admirably filled the mayoress's role.

Educated at Charterhouse School, Godalming, he entered the office

51

of Messrs. Garlick, Park and Sykes, civil engineers, the firm in which his father was a partner. During this period, he was employed on the Ribble surveys in connection with the Preston Corporation projects for the construction of the docks. In August, 1887, he became a partner in the firm Park and Son.

For a number of years he was a member of the Lancashire County Council and besides serving on numerous public bodies he was actively involved with the Royal Lancashire Agricultural Society, being the honorary showyard director from 1901 to 1908. He also played his part in the Preston Guild Show in 1902.

After the death of his second wife, he disposed of his house in Preston and from 1912 onwards, he lived principally in Crowborough, Sussex. He married for a third time, the daughter of William Perrin of Rocklands Stillorgan, Dublin.

During the summer of 1922, he was staying at the Grosvenor Hotel in London, in the company of his third wife. He had become obsessed with his financial state — although he should have been secure enough after the sale of his property in Preston and from the proceeds of his second wife's estate. Nevertheless he wrote to a long standing solicitor friend, asking him to find him a job, stating his finances were very, very bad.

While he dwelt on his problems, he asked his wife to visit her family in Ireland, while he sorted out his affairs.

In the middle of August, he left the Grosvenor Hotel and went to stay at the Bray Mead Court Hotel, near Maidenhead. He prolonged his stay into a second week and on Wednesday, he left the hotel to go for a walk. Nothing more was heard of him. That evening, a passenger in one of the Oxford and Kingston steamers reported to the Windsor police that a body had been seen in the shallow water on the Thames above Surley Hall. The Eton police were informed and members of the Eton and Windsor Royal Humane Society searched the river but found no sign of the body.

On the Friday afternoon, a man from Portsmouth, who was staying at Windsor, walked into Eton police station and handed the Inspector on duty an automatic revolver, which was loaded in four chambers, two having been discharged. The man had noticed the revolver in the water while he was fishing. He got it out of the river and while wiping it he had accidentally touched the trigger and almost shot himself in the leg.

Following this revelation a search was made of the section of the river, and eventually a body was found floating face downwards about four yards from the bank and close to where the revolver had been found. The body, entangled in weeds, was that of Philip Park. Following its recovery a bullet wound was found in the head.

At the inquest which followed it was stated that a search of the deceased man's bedroom at the hotel had produced a note which read:

"Please communicate with my wife Mrs. Philip Park c/o William Perrin Esq., Rocklands, Stillorgan, Co. Dublin. The rest of my luggage is at the Grosvenor Hotel, London. My brain is on fire and I feel mad. I have been living in hell for the past two years. P. Park."

According to the police inspector, called to give evidence, the theory was that the deceased had stood in shallow water and shot himself and that the body had then floated downstream.

The financial affairs of Mr. Park were discussed and as he was a most faithful and affectionate husband who had no reputation for drinking or gambling, it was difficult to imagine how he could have squandered his wealth. Reference was made to a letter he wrote to his wife over in Ireland and in this he stated that his brain was in a whirl.

The sentence in his final note: "I have been living in hell for two years", was a mystery to the witnesses called and the only conclusion drawn was that it referred to his financial position.

At the conclusion of proceedings, the jury at the inquest delivered a verdict that Philip Samuel Park had "Committed Suicide While Temporarily Insane".

Double Killing in Avenham Road

ON 20th August, 1925, Dr. W.H. Pimblett was called by Mrs. Beatrice Brooks to her home, 29 Grimshaw Street, to examine her husband, Walter Brooks, a market salesman. He had been suffering from delusions about his wife's conduct and had been making threats towards her. Following examination, the doctor was greatly concerned about the man's state of mind. He immediately decided that Walter Brooks was insane and he made out a three day detention order, which he instructed Mrs. Brooks to hand to a relieving officer, who would in turn

Avenham Road. As the Town Hall clock struck 10.15 on the spring evening of April 4th, 1928, Beatrice Brooks and Alfred Moore left their lodgings in Avenham Road to meet an untimely end by the gun-weilding Walter Brooks.

have him removed to a detention ward at Fulwood, prior to removal to an asylum.

So concerned was the Doctor with the seriousness of the case, that he visited the house twice the next day to see whether the detention order had been carried out only to find Mrs. Brooks insisting that her husband was much quieter and had therefore decided to give him another chance.

The couple's relationship, however, continued to be a stormy one and on a number of occasions Walter Brooks threatened his wife's well-being. Eventually in October, 1927, they separated, when she went to live at 39 Avenham Road, Preston.

Even after the separation, the estranged husband continued to pursue his wife, which usually ended in jealous quarrels.

Eventually on the night of April 4th, 1928, the troubled relationship had a tragic end. At about 10.15 that evening, shots were heard in Avenham Road and Walter Brooks was seen limping away. Beatrice Brooks, aged 48, was found dead on the footpath and close by in the roadway was Alfred Moore, aged 50, who lodged at the same address. Both had been shot by a revolver belonging to Walter Brooks.

The unfortunate Mr. Moore died on the way to the Infirmary and Mrs. Brooks passed away later the same evening.

At the trial of 48-year-old Walter Brooks, which was held at Manchester Assizes, there was little doubt as to his guilt concerning the double killing but his defence lawyers put great faith in their ability to prove his insanity.

The visit of Dr. Pimblett to his home in August, 1925, and the resultant attempt to have him certified insane was recalled. It was also stated how, in 1924, he had been involved in a serious motor accident. His daughter Blanche Victoria Brooks told how he had been kept in the Infirmary for a long time after the accident. She also told the Court that, although before the accident her father had not behaved well to her mother, his behaviour had been much worse afterwards. She also related how he had constantly threatened her and accused her of misbehaviour with other men, allegations which were completely untrue.

Also revealed was the fact that the prisoner's family had a history of insanity, with one of his brothers having died in Winwick Asylum, in 1907 and another brother having died in Queen's Park Hospital, Blackburn, in 1912, after being diagnosed insane.

Friends and acquaintances of the prisoner gave evidence of their

experience of him and recalled his alleged catalogue of complaints about his wife; his occasional demented condition and his heavy drinking. Brooks himself, blamed his heavy drinking on the fact that he could not sleep without it.

The defence counsel stressed the fact that if the detention certificate of August, 1925, had been acted upon then the terrible tragedy would have been avoided. Even so the jury found Walter Brooks "Guilty" of the double murder and Mr. Justice Charles passed the sentence of death on the prisoner. An appeal was lodged and while it was pending, the condemned man was examined by three eminent mental experts on behalf of the Home

If the advice had been acted upon, of Dr. W.H. Pimblett (above) to have Walter Brooks "certified insane" in 1925, the double tragedy in April 1928 would have been avoided.

Secretary. Nothing was found to alter the Court's verdict and the appeal was dismissed.

A petition was next drawn up and many Prestonians added their signatures to it but this was also dismissed by the Home Secretary who stated there was no reason for advising His Majesty to interfere with the course of the law.

The execution of Walter Brooks took place on the last Thursday in June, 1928, at eight o'clock in the morning, at Strangeways Gaol, Manchester. Outside the prison gates a crowd of about 150 spectators waited in silence for the tolling of the bell and posting of the official notices. The grim task was carried out by Executioner Pierpoint, who despatched the double killer from this life with swift efficiency.

Dreadful Murder in Peel Hall Street

IN the spring of 1877, James Summershall was lodging at the provision shop of Mr. & Mrs. Shaw in Peel Hall Street, Preston, as he had done for the previous nine or ten years.

James Shaw was a picture-frame maker employed at the Church Street establishment of a Mr. Parker. Mrs. Shaw worked as a weaver at Sharples Mill. The couple had a baby daughter, Elizabeth, and they and their lodger gave the child much affection.

Summershall, who had been separated from his wife for a long time, was regarded as a steady character, except when he went on a drinking spree and unfortunately drinking had started to become a regular occurrence. He worked as a fitter and when not affected by drink, was regarded as a first class workman at his place of employment, Messrs. Atherton in North Road.

From the start of the new year, he had not been happy in his work and it was felt his situation was aggravated by his excessive drinking. He was a non-unionist worker and over a few weeks, he developed the belief that members of the union were watching him, and desired to have him sent to a lunatic asylum.

The consequence of this, at the beginning of March, was that he handed in his notice to quit his employment. From that time he had an air of despondency about him and appeared to go thin and nervous with a look of anxiety. He complained to his landlady of pains in the head and told her that several times lately he had been followed and watched by large numbers of people. This same hallucination, he also told to a local pastor. He began to while-away his hours by studying most earnestly, a copy of the Bible.

On Sunday, 18th March, at around 10 o'clock, Mr. & Mrs. Shaw left their Peel Hall Street home to attend a service at Lancaster Road Independent Chapel.

Summershall remained at the provision shop along with the 11-month-old baby Elizabeth, together with the child's grandmother. While the grandmother was in the process of cleaning the house and preparing dinner, the lodger was playing with, and amusing the child. As usual Summershall exhibited much affection and love for the child.

At about twelve o'clock the child began to cry, then grandmother, in her usual good-natured manner, knowing how to humour Summershall, said she would make him a comfortable seat in the corner. She did so, then gave him back the infant to nurse, which he did for some minutes; the child appearing highly delighted.

Summershall then carried the child into the shop and through the windows in the shop door drew the child's attention to her grandmother, who clapped her hands and amused her for a minute. The grandmother then turned her back and went out of the rear door to empty some 'slops'.

When she came back into the house she heard Summershall rush out of the shop door and she immediately thought he had run out with the child. Naturally she was greatly alarmed and ran out of the house to see where he had gone to. She could not find them, but she did see her son coming down Peel Hall Street and asked him had he seen the lodger, for he had run off with the child.

Mr. Shaw replied that Summershall had passed him at great speed in Meadow Street and that he had no child with him at the time. "He must have taken it somewhere", the grandmother replied, "He had been holding her in the shop prior to his leaving the premises". Her son then suggested he had perhaps put the child down somewhere and then left. At once a search was begun. The mother and father had by now arrived, and all searched the kitchen and yard for the infant. The grandmother, meanwhile checked in the shop. Then to her horror behind the counter a most awful and sickening sight met her gaze. The child lay there with blood pouring from a gaping wound in her throat. Death had been instantaneous. Three fingers and a thumb on the right hand were also cut, which suggested that the little child had tried in vain to save herself.

Information was immediately sent to the police and prior to their arrival, a little boy who lived next door, had come into the house and on looking into the child's cradle, saw a large knife with marks of blood on the blade. The knife, which was long and sharp, was the one which usually lay on the shop counter and was used in the business.

Meanwhile, Summershall, who had passed Mr. Shaw in Meadow Street arrived at the local police station. Breathlessly, he told the duty inspector that he had just killed a child to save himself. "To save yourself, from whom?", inquired the inspector. To which Summershall, behaving in a very distracted manner, replied: "There are hundreds after me".

Soon afterwards details of the horrible murder reached the police station. All doubt was immediately set at rest, as the truthfulness of the man's statement became apparent. He was at once locked up and placed under strict guard, for his condition was such that it was feared he would attempt to end his own life.

News of the crime spread with alarming rapidity through the town and neighbourhood. Throughout the remainder of the day a continual stream of people passed up and down the street and great excitement prevailed.

Meadow Street. As James Shaw made his way home along Meadow Street, he met his lodger James Summershall who was running the opposite way. Summershall said he was running after another man.

Persons who were acquainted with Summershall generally thought that he had committed the dreadful act of butchery while in a state of mental aberration which had come upon him quite suddenly and impelled him irresistibly to the crime. He was known to have been very fond of the child and often made it a special pastime to play with her on coming home from work in an evening.

He did have a history of violent behaviour, however, which usually manifested itself when he was in an intoxicated state. Apparently on one occasion he had attempted to stab a couple of people in Burnley and as a consequence of this had been imprisoned for a short term.

The following day the prisoner was brought before the magistrates of the borough and a coroner's inquest was held at the police station. Summershall described as about five feet seven inches tall, of sallow complexion and wearing a moustache, was charged with the 'Wilful Murder' of the baby girl.

During the inquiry, Summershall was accommodated on a chair in the dock and conducted himself in a calm manner. The grim details of the previous day's tragedy were recalled and various witnesses gave evidence of the prisoner's actions that day and over the previous weeks.

The coroner's jury retired to consider their verdict and within a minute were back in court with a verdict of "Guilty" against James Summershall. The coroner then asked the prisoner if he had anything to say and he replied: "I wish to say it was wilful, I was not out of my mind altogether, only I was excited". The coroner then informed him that he would be formally committed to take his trial at the next Lancaster Assizes.

The Assizes took place in July, 1877, and when charged with 'Wilful Murder', Summershall pleaded "Not Guilty".

As the grim details yet again unfolded it was proved beyond doubt, that the prisoner had ended the life of the unfortunate infant.

Great importance was placed on the medical evidence concerning the state of mind of the accused. The doctor, who had examined him shortly after the killing, declared that he had in his time seen a great many lunatics and that from his experience he had no hesitation in coming to the conclusion that the prisoner was insane.

The jury subsequently returned a verdict to the effect that the prisoner was Guilty of Murder, but that at the time of the act, was not responsible for his actions. Acting on this decision, His Lordship ordered Summershall to be detained During Her Majesty's Pleasure.

Insanity Drove Husband to Kill

AT around one o'clock on a Saturday afternoon in May, 1842, the peace of Vicar Street, situated close to Trinity Church was disturbed by the appearance of Sarah Whittle at the front door of her home. Her hand was covering her throat from which blood was streaming. With her was her mother-in-law and their terrifying cries alerted the neighbourhood to a terrible tragedy.

As they stood at the doorstep another scream was heard from the vicinity of the kitchen. That cry came from Peter Whittle who having slit the throat of his wife, was endeavouring to end his own life in similar fashion. Whilst sitting in a kitchen chair he had run the razor across his own neck, which he intended as the final action of a most mystifying crime which seemed to have no motive for its enactment.

Trinity Parish Church as it was in the early 19th century (it was demolished in 1951 and the parish merged with that of St. George). It stood near to Vicar Street, where in May 1842, Sarah Whittle appeared at the door of her home with her throat cut.

Just a few minutes earlier, the couple, his mother and the two children of their seven-year marriage, had dined together in apparent harmony. That morning, Sarah Whittle had been working at a mill in Pitt Street, where they were both employed as cotton spinners. Her intention had been to return for an afternoon shift, and they were together in the parlour prior to her intended departure. His mother, busying herself in the kitchen, was alerted by the noise of something falling. When she entered the parlour she saw her son with his arm around his wife, who appeared to be in a fainting state. They had their backs to his mother and when they turned round she saw Sarah with blood pouring from her neck. Peter Whittle said nothing as the woman came to the aid of her daughter-in-law.

At once, the local constable was alerted and along with medical assistance, they were soon on the scene. Of the two, the wife was in a most serious condition, her head having been almost severed from her body. Within minutes of the surgeon's arrival she was dead. A number of cuts on her hands suggested that she had put up a struggle to prevent the premature end of her life of just 28 years.

Peter Whittle, who had remained in the kitchen, was then administered to by the surgeon and was removed to the House of Recovery. Little hope was given of his survival but gradually after a few days, his condition improved.

By the time of the Lancaster Mid-summer Assizes of the same year, Whittle was considered recovered enough to stand trial on the charge of Wilful Murder.

It was stated that the unfortunate couple had lived with the accused's parents throughout their marriage and to all observations they had appeared to be an affectionate twosome. Sarah Whittle had, at the time of her death, been expecting their third child and was said to have been about five months pregnant.

Witnesses testified that for a few months prior to the tragedy, her husband had appeared to be in low spirits. His mother recalled how he had been complaining of pains in his head and of being generally unwell, and a rash had developed on his body which had increased his low feelings.

Whittle was not a man who indulged in much drinking and had shown great affection for his children. The general belief was that the family did not quarrel and lived on happy terms.

When all the evidence had been concluded the defence counsel reminded the jury of the couple's affectionate partnership and suggested to them that the prisoner had to be labouring under temporary insanity to commit such a crime. There had been no reason, he added, for the prisoner to have attacked his wife and then to have attempted to take his own life unless labouring under some positive delusion. In fact he claimed he had been driven to the fatal deed by "nervous excitement" and his own bodily illness. There was, he concluded, no motive whatsoever for the terrible crime that he perpetrated.

The jury then retired to consider their verdict and returned into court after a long deliberation. The verdict they arrived at was "Not Guilty", they being of the opinion that at the time of the killing Peter Whittle was insane. That decision meant that the loving father from Vicar Street was destined to spend the rest of his life in a 'Suitable Place of Confinement'.

The Brutal Slaying of Ann Gilligan

ON Monday, 4th June, 1866, Ann Gilligan, the wife of a private in the 36th Regiment, entered the Arkwright Arms at the bottom of Stoneygate, in the company of a man named John Banks. The woman was a well-known local prostitute and for about twelve months she had been cohabiting with her companion.

It was about ten thirty in the evening when they entered the public house and the woman ordered a couple of glasses of ale, for which she paid. The pair sat together in the main room of the establishment.

Some five minutes later the attention of the room's other occupants was aroused when Banks in a raised voice accused his companion of having taken some money out of his pockets. She denied the accusa-

The Arkwright Arms (left) in the 19th century and as the building appears today — now Arkwright House. It was here on Monday, June 4th, 1866, that John Banks embarked on a night of violence which ended in the murder of prostitute, Ann Gilligan.

tion and the man immediately hit her on the head with his fist, and knocked her down on the floor.

As she lay there, Banks started to kick her and only the intervention of witnesses prevented him from administering further punishment. The woman appeared to be little harmed and the pair then returned to their seats and the public house back to normality. A little later the landlord prepared to close for the night and requested the couple and the other remaining customers to leave.

On the way back to their lodging house in Turks Head Yard, the couple resumed their hostilities and various witnesses saw Banks ill-treating the unfortunate woman. When they arrived at the lodging house, another resident heard the screams of Ann Gilligan outside. She was heard to say: "Oh John, don't kill me; have mercy on me". She then fell to the ground and Banks delivered a couple of punches.

Once inside the house he continued to ill-treat her and dragged her up the stairs by the hairs of her head. He accused her of taking 2s. out of his pocket and having spent it. She asked him to leave her alone, and he replied to her: "I will kill you before I have done with you".

When a neighbouring female tried to intervene Banks rounded on her and warned: "If you don't get away, I'll serve you the same".

The disturbance lasted until about three o'clock in the morning when the female lodger, who had an adjoining room, was awoken by Ann Gilligan's screams. She attempted to assist the unfortunate woman and had asked Banks several times if he was going to murder her and he said: "Yes, I will if she does not behave herself differently; she does nothing but drink".

By the morning the battering inflicted on Ann Gilligan had taken its toll and when a neighbour entered the house she found her cuddled up on some straw with her hands and face covered in blood. Banks was not in the house and the local constabulary were immediately alerted.

Medical assistance was soon at hand and Ann Gilligan was immediately taken to the workhouse. She complained of very great pains in her bowels and there were a great number of bruises on her face and hands.

That Tuesday evening, the Borough Magistrate attended the workhouse to obtain a statement from the woman. In it she told how Banks had been in the habit of fighting and kicking her. Going on to relate the terrible punishment that he had inflicted on her the previous night, after accusing her of taking his money.

By ten o'clock that night the 29-year-old girl was dead — her final hours being passed in considerable suffering.

Following her death, John Banks was taken into custody and charged with murdering her. After being cautioned he said: "I didn't murder her; she was drunk. I was trying to carry her upstairs when she slipped out of my arms, and fell downstairs. She had been drinking all day".

Later at the inquest Banks was committed to take his trial at the next Lancaster Assizes on the charge of Wilful Murder.

When the Assizes took place in July, 1866, Mr. Baron Martin presided over the case which had aroused much interest in Preston and the surrounding districts.

The terrible tale of violence was once again related and at the end of the prosecution's case the learned counsel said the only conclusion he could come to was that the prisoner knew perfectly well what he was doing.

The prisoner's counsel stated that in his opinion it was another addition to the long list of horrors that had been caused by drink. He claimed it was no premeditated action but an act carried out under the stimulating influence of alcohol.

When the judge summed up he told the jury that the only question was whether they believed the evidence submitted. If they believed it, he added, then it was their duty to find the prisoner guilty of murder and not manslaughter.

The jury then retired to consider their verdict and after an absence of ten minutes, they returned into Court, with a verdict of "Guilty of Wilful Murder".

The judge, amidst breathless silence, put on the black cap and addressing John Banks said the jury had found him guilty of murder and upon the evidence it would have been utterly impossible for them to have found any other verdict. He was guilty, the judge continued, of the most barbarous violence both in the house and on the way home. He then proceeded to pass the sentence of death on the 34-year-old labourer. As he read out the sentence His Lordship displayed great emotion, and at times was scarcely able to proceed.

The prisoner, a rather stout-built and powerful looking man of moderate height, had maintained a stolid indifference throughout the trial. He was then removed from the dock.

In the following days a petition was forwarded to the Home Office in the hope of having the sentence commuted to one of Penal Servitude

For Life. A reply to the plea arrived at his Preston solicitors on 6th August, 1866. It read:

> "Sir — The Secretary of State for the Home Department, has considered the case of John Banks, on whose behalf you have applied to him. I have the satisfaction to acquaint you that he has felt warranted, under all the circumstances, in advising Her Majesty to commute the capital sentence into Penal Servitude For Life.
> I am your obedient servant,   H. Waddington."

The news that the convict had been reprieved created much satisfaction at Lancaster, as it saved the town from the revolting spectacle of a public execution. But the brutality of the circumstances attending the murder caused many people to be surprised at the granting of the reprieve.

Postscript on Ann Gilligan

At the time of the case, discussions were taking place in the House of Lords with a view to abolishing the death sentence for murder in the second degree, that is, where there had been no premeditation. Doubtless the commutation of Bank's sentence had been occasioned by the absence of premeditation.

Dispute Over a Dog

AT the Lancaster Spring Assizes of 1869, a 22-year-old weaver named John Caton, appeared before Mr. Justice Denman, charged with the murder of Jane Waterhouse. The alleged victim of John Caton was a 58-year-old woman of frail appearance, who, like the accused, lived in Crown Street, Preston.

At about three o'clock in the afternoon, on 23rd February, the accused and two other men were seen walking along Crown Street in the direction of the woman's house. On reaching the house, Caton said to the other men: "This is the house" and climbed the steps to the front door. He seized the latch and on finding that the door did not yield, he placed his knee against it and burst it open. He then hastily entered and within a couple of minutes, witnesses in the street heard a scream and saw the woman, Jane Waterhouse, rush out of the front door and down the steps followed by Caton, who had, by then, a dog under his arm. As he pursued her he took a running punch at her, hitting her in the ribs with his clogged foot. The poor woman staggered forward and fell to her knees.

The woman's husband was now in the street and rushed towards Caton. He successfully knocked him to the ground and at this point, two other men, who had been in the company of Caton, came to his aid and pulled the distraught husband off him. Caton, with the dog in his possesion, then went home. A couple of women who had witnessed the incidents then helped Jane Waterhouse to her home.

Apparently the argument had been over the dog, a greyhound of Italian breed. Caton had claimed that the animal was his, although Mrs. Waterhouse maintained that it had been given to her by another person.

At about nine o'clock that evening a local surgeon called to see Jane Waterhouse and she was lying in bed downstairs. He found her in a state of collapse and on examination he discovered that the tenth rib on her right hand side was broken. She seemed to be suffering greatly. From then on he visited her daily until Tuesday, 3rd March, when she died in the early hours of the morning.

The following day a post mortem examination took place. This showed that the lung tissue had been perforated by the fractured rib. Prior to the incident, the woman had been suffering from consolidation of the lungs and from the surgeon's examination, he stated that he would not have been surprised had she died from this complaint itself within a few weeks. He also stated the fact that the skin in the area of the fracture was not discoloured, suggesting that the kick inflicted was only a slight one.

Some four days after the incident took place, Caton was charged with violently assaulting Jane Waterhouse, and a few days before her death, was present when local justices took a deposition from the woman.

In this, Mrs. Waterhouse spoke of Caton entering her house and getting hold of the dog. Of his kicking her on the shin, and of her running into the street where he punched her in the ribs, causing her to fall to her knees.

Caton then accused her of getting hold of a poker and hitting him on the head, a charge which she denied. In fact examination of Caton showed no sign of receiving such a blow and the only injuries he had received appeared to be as a result of the skirmish with the deceased woman's husband, after his assault on her. Witnesses called to testify, told of threats that Caton had made to the woman's well-being, including the remark that he would "Either have the dog or her life".

When all the trial evidence had been submitted His Lordship delivered a lengthy summing up. He told them that the prisoner had come to the Assizes on the charge of manslaughter and not murder. However after perusing the depositions in the case, he felt that there was not a scrap of evidence of any sort on which he felt himself warranted in ordering a bill for manslaughter to be sent up before the grand jury.

He then went on to say that in his opinion the case appeared to be one of deliberate, cruel, excessive and brutal violence, by a young strong man, upon an old and feeble woman.

Concerning the animal at the centre of the incident, he remarked that whether or not the dog belonged to the prisoner, there was no justification in him entering the woman's house with violent hands or violent feet to injure her in order to posses himself of the property. If the woman's death had been accelerated by the prisoner's cruelty, although she was in a feeble state of health at the time, the offence was nonetheless murder or manslaughter, as the case maybe.

The summing up completed, the jury retired and returned after fifteen minutes deliberation. In reply to the usual question from the Clerk of the Crown the foreman of the jury said they had found the prisoner "Guilty of Wilful Murder", though they strongly and unanimously recommended him to mercy.

The prisoner, who was terribly excited was asked by the Clerk of the Crown, if he had anything to say and he replied: "Gentleman, I could call witnesses including the two men with me in Crown Street, who will testify that I never said I would have her life".

His Lordship interrupted the prisoner saying that it was impossible to wait for other witnesses. The trial was over, and he had been found guilty on the clearest possible evidence indeed, and wholly independent of that expression, of a deliberate brutal murder.

The prisoner tried to interrupt again but His Lordship continued, stating there would be no mercy for the accused. The jury's recommendation would be forwarded to the proper quarter, he added, whether it would be attended to or not, he would not for one moment say.

His Lordship, without donning the black cap, pronounced the death sentence, ending with the words: "May the Lord have mercy on your soul".

The prisoner was then removed from the dock, wringing his hands piteously. The sentence passed, Caton kept his eyes fixed doggedly on the ground.

As soon as word reached Preston that John Caton had been sentenced to the gallows, steps were immediately taken with a view to obtaining a remission of the sentence. It was thought by many persons in the Borough that Penal Servitude For Life was a more suitable sentence. With this in mind, a petition was drawn- up for the Home Secretary. A few days later a communication was received from the Home Secretary, stating that a command from the Queen had ordered a respite of the execution of the sentence.

Brutal Murder in Brown Street

DURING October, 1838, Michael Donohoe, a gangsman or sub-contractor, arrived in Preston from Ireland, to supervise a gang of Irish labourers working on the North Union Railway development. Donohoe was described as a 40-year-old man of good character, steady and respectable who had left his wife and children at home in Ireland.

He took up lodgings with the Lacky family in Brown Street, a small narrow street near to Marsh Lane. The street was at the time principally inhabited by Irish labourers and other residents who were also employed by the railway.

Altogether, about 20 labourers were in Donohoe's charge. One of his duties each Saturday was to pay them for the week's work. In the last week of November, for some inexplicable reason, he did not pay them on the Saturday and it was the following Monday evening before he set-about the task.

Along with a colleague, he firstly went to the Bay Horse at Penwortham, where he paid four workmen, before then proceeding to Brown Street, where the bulk of his employees lived. Once there he went to the home of James Lacky and his wife, Julia, where he lodged. At the house was Michael and Patrick Lacky, brothers of James Lacky, and several other workmen, to receive the money outstanding to them.

Donohoe announced to the men that he would not pay them until he had settled an account with Julia Lacky for some provisions she had purchased for the men, on his behalf, during the previous week.

Julia Lacky then went to the nearby provisions shop and returned with a bill which was undated. He suspected it to be a forged one and demanded that the woman take it back and have it dated. She was infuriated by his remarks and angrily replied with the words: "I'll have the bill kicked out of him before he leaves the house".

Her husband, James Lacky, then uttered a similar threat and then spoke to his brothers, Michael and Patrick and said: "Go out and fetch a few boys, and then we'll either kick the life out of him or kick the head off him and make him pay".

Julia, Patrick and Michael Lacky then left the house. They returned a few minutes later accompanied by a dozen or so other men. All stood silent for a little while and then Julia Lacky said she would go and fetch another bill. After she had gone, Mr. Donohoe's colleague, a worried witness of the threatening scene, sent for the assistance of the local constable. Some ten minutes after her departure, Julia Lacky returned with a bill which was suitably dated and claimed £2. 17s. 9d. owing for the provisions. At that stage two constables appeared and all seemed quite amicable among the parties and they then left with the impression that the matter had been satisfactorily resolved.

The time was now close to eight o'clock and Donohoe was left in the house alone with the Lackys and the other Irish labourers. Within minutes cries of: "Mercy", "Murder" and "Robbery" were heard coming from the house. When anxious neighbours tried to enter the premises, the door was bolted.

Shortly afterwards all the occupants, except for the unfortunate Donohoe, were seen leaving the house by the back door, which was locked after them as they fled into the night.

The police, alerted by neighbours, who had been horrified by the cries and shrieks coming from the house, arrived back on the scene. They forced the front door open and the first sight that greeted them was the lifeless corpse of the ill fated Donohoe. He was huddled in a kind of double sitting position in a corner of the room with a pool of blood surrounding him. A mangled, disfigured and mutilated figure on the stone flags was the outcome of a merciless and ruthless killing carried out by his fellow countrymen. A search of the body revealed that his assailants had taken from his waistcoat pocket the money in his possession.

Not surprisingly, this dreadful killing stunned the residents of Brown Street and the Irish community that inhabited the town. The feelings of horror of people in the area were so strong at the time that several who resided near the "house of blood" left their premises and could not be persuaded to return.

Despite an unremitting search to locate the Lackys and other persons who were supposed to have participated in the dreadful deed, no trace of them could be found and it was concluded that they had all left the town.

The post mortem examination took place under the supervision of Dr. St. Clare, an eminent local physician. The principal wound was a deep incision which penetrated the scalp immediately above the left eye. This wound had been inflicted by a sharp weapon with great force because it extended some distance through the scalp into the brain.

On the top of the head there was a deep and dangerous cut which appeared to have been caused by a blunt instrument, while several bruises on the body were consistent with the victim being kicked. The terrible picture was completed by marks around the neck and throat which suggested an attempt at strangulation.

The inquest was held in the Town Hall and details of the sordid affair were revealed by the superintendent of the police, who informed the assembled gathering that in a few days further evidence would be forthcoming.

The endeavours of the police were partly successful when James Lacky and his wife were taken into custody, after being discovered in Liverpool.

Physician William St. Clare, (above) was called to Brown Street in November, 1838, to find Michael Donohoe stretched upon the floor "quite dead".

The Town Hall was packed for the resumption of the inquest, with many of the town's most respectable inhabitants in attendance. What unfolded was a terrible tale of cruel and ruthless murder, of which the Lackys had played the major role.

Once both the medical and circumstantial evidence had been presented, the coroner summed up the proceedings and the jury retired. Some twenty minutes later they returned to deliver a verdict of "Wilful Murder" against James Lacky, Patrick Lacky, Michael Lacky, Julia Lacky and other persons whose names were unknown. The coroner then made out a warrant for the committal of the prisoners for trial at Lancaster Castle.

Concerning the missing brothers, it was stated that they had accompanied James and Julia Lacky to Liverpool after the killing and then had taken lodgings there; keeping themselves closely concealed. The day before the two were apprehended, both Patrick and Michael Lacky had gone away.

When the case against James and Julia Lacky subsequently came up for trial at Lancaster Spring Assizes, the Court was informed that key witnesses had not appeared. His Lordship then informed the gathering that the trial must be postponed until the next Assizes and the accused be confined until that time.

Eventually, in August, 1839, 29-year-old James Lacky and his 21-year-old wife, Julia, stood trial at Lancaster for the Brown Street murder of November, 1838. The evidence against the pair was most conclusive. The brutal manner in which Donohoe was slaughtered was revealed once again.

The prosecution attempted to include the depositions of the two witnesses who had still not been traced but this action was objected to by the defence counsel.

In the prisoner's defence it was claimed that the evidence produced had not proved that either of the two accused had delivered any mortal blow. The claim was that a general scuffle had taken place and that the deceased had been brutally kicked by some of the strong and healthy ruffians who quarrelled with him, and not by the prisoners. In fact, the defence counsel argued that James Lacky was a man in a weak and sickly state and therefore not likely to have been the one to inflict such

The Dungeons, Lancaster Castle, where James and Julia Lacky were incarcerated before "transportation beyond the seas for the rest of their natural lives".

vicious blows. Finally he urged the jury to give the prisoners the benefit of any doubt.

The learned judge then briefly summed-up the evidence and the jury, after their deliberations, found both the prisoners "Guilty of Manslaughter". His Lordship, in passing sentence, said the jury had taken a most merciful view of their case and looking at all the circumstances, he had no hesitation as to the sentence which he should pronounce — which would be the most severe which the law imposed for the crime of which they had been convicted.

James Lacky then spoke out, crying: "Oh! Mercy, mercy, my Lord".

"I cannot forget", said his Lordship, "that when that unfortunate man, whom you hurried into eternity cried to you, James Lacky, for mercy, he cried in vain. The sentence of the Court is, that you, and each of you be transported beyond the seas for the term of your natural lives".

The prisoner James Lacky then repeatedly exclaimed "Oh my Lord, my Lord, let us go together". The female prisoner, a very pretty young woman, fell on her knees, shrieking: "Oh my children, my poor children, what will become of them". She continued repeating these exclamations as she was removed from the dock.

The Preston Bank Swindler

GERALD Thomas Tully entered the Preston Bank, now the Midland Bank, in Fishergate, as a junior clerk. In 1866 he was appointed sub-manager. When his chief retired in 1883, Tully applied for the post of bank manager. The board, however, was concerned about Tully's high spending lifestyle and hints that he gambled. Another man was given the post and Tully seemed to accept the situation.

The Preston Bank (now Midland Bank), Fishergate, from an early 19th century engraving. it was here that Gerald Thomas Tully was employed before catching a train at Preston Station to begin an amazing 19th century transatlantic tale.

With the change in management came the usual searching audit when customers' balances and security deeds were examined. On the morning of the audit, Tully slipped quietly out of the bank and made his way down Fishergate to the railway station, where he was spotted by friends boarding a train bound for Manchester.

His wife received a letter from him bearing a Manchester postmark saying he was on business for a few days. He also wrote to the bank stating that he would return the next day.

Meanwhile the bank discovered that defalcations of around

£10,000, equivalent to over a quarter of a million pounds by today's values. Nothing more was heard of Tully's whereabouts. Rumours abounded that he had made his way to one of Europe's leading cities. A warrant was issued for his arrest but the search for him proved fruitless — until 16th May, 1884.

At the time, Preston magistrate, councillor Joseph Toulmin, whose family had founded the *Lancashire Evening Post*, was in New York with his wife for the purpose of visiting relatives. As the couple strolled down Broadway, Mr. Toulmin caught sight of a man in front walking with a familiar swaggering style.

"Why that's Tully", exclaimed Mr. Toulmin, and he called out his name. The man turned round coolly raised his hat and replied: "I beg your pardon sir but my name is Richardson". Undeterred Mr. & Mrs. Toulmin followed the man until they saw a police officer. The couple explained to the officer who he was and the fact that he was a wanted criminal.

The officer took the man into custody, despite his protests that he was from Birmingham and not Preston. Transatlantic communication was made and Preston police sent a photograph of Tully to the New York police. There was no mistaking the likeness, so he was kept in custody. When his possessions were searched a loan ticket bearing the name of a firm in Lune Street, Preston, was discovered. Unfortunately due to a legal loophole, which was later amended, the British Government failed to get Tully extradited. Having been held for three months, the New York authorities had no option but to release the Preston Bank swindler. For a time afterwards he remained in New York and then he moved to Chicago.

A Preston police officer, who visited Tully during his confinement, revealed to him that his wife and son had gone to live in Manchester in distressing circumstances.

The next time the townsfolk of Preston heard of the former deputy manager of the Preston Bank was a report of his death in the *Preston Guardian* in April, 1888. A communication had been received that he had died in Chicago and been interred in the cemetery there on 23rd March, 1888.

Postscript on the Preston Bank Swindler

In his time at the Preston Bank, Tully had been regarded as a pillar of society and had lived with his family in the fashionable West Cliff

Terrace. His embezzlement and his escape from justice was a much talked-about subject during the latter years of the 19th century. Despite a new name and a new lifestyle and his escape from justice, he could not change his swaggering walk, which eventually led to his discovery.

Double Death in Albert Road

JAMES Brocklebank Proctor was a 21-year-old man of regular habits, who lived with his parents in Brook Street, Preston. On Sunday, 27th May, 1883, he had not returned home by his usual 10 o'clock in the evening and his father was feeling somewhat uneasy about his non-appearance. At half-past ten a knock on the door brought a visitor who relayed to the parents sad news of their son and his girl-friend — 20-year-old Mary Yates. What was revealed was one of the saddest tragedies that had darkened the streets of Preston for some years.

The young solicitor's clerk had met his sweetheart, a domestic servant, in the early part of the evening and they had spent their time walking the streets of Fulwood. A number of people who recognised the couple saw them walking together during the evening. Shortly after 9 o'clock they were seen heading along Albert Road. Things did not seem to be exactly harmonious and the girl was seen once or twice to leave her companion. Then, according to witnesses on the other side of the road, Proctor was seen to take out a revolver and shoot the girl. He immediately afterwards raised the revolver to his own head and shot himself.

A crowd rapidly gathered and medical assistance was soon on hand. The body of Proctor was slumped in a hedgerow and Mary Yates lay on the footpath only yards from her killer. She was not at this stage dead and was removed to the Fulwood hospital. Her father, James Yates, a drainer of Broughton was immediately informed and he rushed to the hospital where he remained until she passed away in the early hours of the morning, never regaining consciousness.

At the inquest into the tragedy, details of the couple's romance were discussed in an attempt to unravel the mystery of their untimely deaths. They had been keeping company for about three years and some seven months before her death, Mary Yates had spoken of her impending wedding to James Proctor. For about five years she had worked as a domestic servant in the employ of Mr. Wilding of Sunny Bank, Fulwood and had left with her marriage looming. Albeit at the time the intended nuptials were delayed and while she waited, acquired a similar position in the home of Mr. Knagg, a schoolmaster, of Grosvenor Terrace.

Proctor had continued to pay attention to the girl as previously and they were frequently seen together. The girl had previously confided to her mistress that she was to be married soon and that she was happy in her courtship, and that her lover was both respectable and steady.

While in the service of Mr. Knagg, the girl was regarded as kind and industrious and was described as a general favourite. She and her fiance were both members of the St. Peters Church bible class and Mr. Knagg, was the teacher in charge of the group. There had been no indication of Proctor's intention to commit such a terrible deed and no witness called had noticed any change in the demeanour of Proctor prior to the incident.

The couple had disagreed at times and it was related that Proctor had been known to take another girl to the theatre on occasions. It was said that at times he had lied to the girl but his motive had been to marry her. However the girl had been advised not to marry him because he had not the means to keep her.

The fact that Proctor had purchased the revolver on 16th April, 1883, from a Preston pawnbroker, suggested that the crime was premeditated. The inquest jury had a short deliberation and came to the conclusion that Mary Ann Yates had met her death by the act of James Brocklebank Proctor, and that he maliciously, feloniously and of malice aforethought, murdered her.

The verdict regarding Proctor was that he wilfully committed suicide with malice aforethought.

On the Wednesday after the killings, the deceased girl was interred in Broughton Churchyard, witnessed by crowds of spectators who had been attracted partly by curiosity and in many cases in great sympathy.

At about eight o'clock the following morning a funeral procession left the house of James Proctor and proceeded to the Church of England portion of the cemetery. Without a religious service, the coffin was lowered into its last resting place before about one hundred onlookers.

The Murder of Bombardier Short

ON 24th April, 1903, Gunner William George Hudson, aged 26, appeared at the Manchester Assizes, accused of the murder of Bombardier Harry Short, at Fulwood Barracks, on the morning of 17th February, 1903. Bombardier Short had been found dead in his bed with a bullet wound in the head.

Owing to the sensational features of the case, desire to gain admission to the Court was keen. Many people from Preston journeyed to Manchester to witness the proceedings. Hudson, who was attired in full dress uniform answered "Not Guilty" when the clerk of the assizes read out the charge.

Both men were members of the Royal Field Artillery. When Gunner

Fulwood Barracks Preston 1990. The impressive stone facade remains little changed in appearance since the time in 1903 when Gunner William George Hudson murdered Bombardier Harry Short.

Hudson had arrived at Fulwood Barracks in December, 1902, he had been placed under the command of Bombardier Short. Gunner Hudson's duties were to see that everything was kept in order and he was assigned a room directly opposite to Bombardier Short's room. Unfortunately, things did not run smoothly and on 27th January, 1903, Bombardier Short made a charge against the prisoner for disobeying orders and for striking him. When the charge was heard on 5th February, Gunner Hudson was acquitted and subsequently moved from his quarters close to Bombardier Short to another block of buildings.

Following his acquittal Gunner Hudson seemed to bear his superior officer ill will and he told other colleagues that he was determined in some manner or other to gain revenge. On 16th February, in the company of two companions, he left the Barracks for a drinking session. They returned at about 11.30 p.m., and all three appeared to have had a considerable amount to drink.

As the men walked around the parade ground to their quarters, Gunner Hudson told his companions: "I'll do for Short", and was only stopped from going to the Bombardier's quarters by the persistence of one of his companions. Eventually Gunner Hudson went to his own quarters, which he shared with one of his drinking friends. As the two men prepared to settle down for the night he repeated his threat.

Bombardier Short had himself been out for the night. His companion, driver Harry Wells, told the trial that they had returned shortly before midnight.

Gunner John Finneran who occupied the same room as the deceased said that at about 12.30 a.m., he was awakened by a noise resembling the discharge of a rifle. He said he called out: "Whatever is that?" On receiving no answer he went back to sleep. He also stated that the room was in darkness and he could not see anything.

The following morning when Harry Wells went to wake Bombardier Short he found him dead in his bed. One of Gunner Hudson's colleagues stated that the accused man had told him "I've done for Short" and showed him how he had committed his deed, by raising the rifle to his shoulder and standing in a shooting position. It was also related how Gunner Hudson knew the exact layout of the Bombardier's room and that he would have been able to locate his bed in the darkness.

At the conclusion of the trial the jury found Hudson "Guilty" but they recommended mercy. The judge, however, Mr. Justice Lawrence, found no reason for compassion and passed the sentence of death.

During his incarceration, the condemned man gave the officers no

Gunner William George Hudson (left) taken from a contemporary artist's court room sketch. He appeared in court in full dress uniform. A native of Birmingham, he had seen service in South Africa and India.

Hudson was said to be familiar with the layout of the barracks room (below), in which Bombardier Short slept. It was concluded that Hudson crept up to the Bombardier's bed in stockinged-feet, knelt down and discharged the gun.

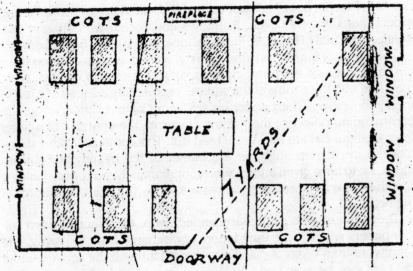

trouble and he displayed great fortitude right up to the end; never denying the justice of his sentence. On the fine morning of 12th May, 1903, a fairly large crowd had gathered early in the vicinity of Strangeways Prison, Manchester, when Gunner William George Hudson was hanged by executioner Billington, at 8 o'clock sharp.

Press representatives were excluded from the execution, but were informed immediately afterwards that everything had passed off satisfactorily — death being "instantaneous". The hoisting of the black flag was by now abolished and the first public sign was a notice posted outside the gate of the prison.

At the inquest it was revealed that William George Hudson had been hanged in plain clothes. The prison authorities had received a note informing them that he had been discharged from the Army a few days before his execution.

Postcript on the Murder of Bombardier Short

Shortly after noon on the day of Hudson's execution a scene took place in the great quadrangle of Fulwood Barracks that was most painful to every military man who took part in it, and also to every civilian who formed part of the spectacular group who fringed the barracks entrance. A communication had been received at the Preston Garrison from General Hallam-Parr of the North-Western District giving orders that Gunners Owen, Matthews and Foster, who all gave evidence at the trial of Gunner Hudson should be expelled from the Army.

The whole of the troops in the garrison were drawn up on three sides of the square and the three gunners, attired in civilian clothes, were marched into the centre of the square, escorted by a squad of men of the Field Artillery. Then under orders from Colonel Sattherwaite, the commanding officer of the Preston Garrison, the contents of a letter from General Hallam-Parr were read out. The communication stated that the three men ought, in the matter of the tragedy at Fulwood Barracks, to have given information sooner than they did, and that they had therefore rendered themselves unworthy to wear the uniform of the regiment.

The gunners, who stood bareheaded, were each then handed yellow papers which were their letters of discharge from the Army. The men were then taken at quick march right through the square, under the barracks gateway and into Watling Street Road. There an ambulance wagon with a canvas cover was waiting and the men were ordered aboard. As one of them nimbly climbed aboard he turned to a khaki-clad soldier who was close by and said: "Goodbye, old Pal". The ambulance, drawn by two horses, was then driven to Preston Railway Station and the discharged men were escorted on to a southbound train.

The Mysterious Murder of James Fell

O N a May morning in 1906, the body of eccentric miser, James Fell, aged 61, was found on the floor of his drysalter's warehouse in St. John's Place, behind Preston Parish Church. He was lying on the floor where he usually slept, covered by a blanket. There were no signs of a struggle and it appeared that he had been murdered while sleeping. A nephew, who worked for Fell, had discovered the body.

A safe stood open but all that was missing was a £5 note and Fell's treasured silver watch. It was believed that the assailant had sneaked inside through a cellar window while Fell was out earlier in the evening, and waited until he went to sleep before attacking him.

It took five months before the police were able to arrest any suspects for the murder. A Martha Whiteside went along to Preston Police Station to give information that led to the eventual arrest of 36-year-old Paddy Callaghan, who had lived with her for a number of years, and also

Two plain-clothes detectives (left) compare notes outside James Fell's warehouse, St. John's Place, after the discovery of his body in the early hours of Saturday, May 19th, 1906.

Tommy "Buck" Beardsworth.

At the trial, at Manchester Assizes, Martha Whiteside said that on 19th May, while she was living apart from Callaghan, he had come to her home and told her that he and Beardsworth had killed Fell in his warehouse. She claimed that she had helped Callaghan burn his bloodstained cap and that she had provided a false alibi for him, during early police enquiries.

Beardsworth maintained that on the night of the killing, he had served in his lock-up Stoneygate tripe shop opposite Arkwright House, until 11 p.m., in the company of Sarah Harris, and that on closing, they had gone to their home in nearby Vauxhall Road. It was stated in Court that the couple, who had lived together for several years, had been hurriedly married, by special licence, at St. James's Church, just a few weeks after the murder. At the trial later, he denied that he had married because of the law that prevented a wife giving evidence against her husband in a murder trial.

Callaghan maintained that he spent the night of the killing with Martha Whiteside, and that she had invented the story to get him into trouble, as their relationship was going through a difficult period and also because he had shown interest in another woman.

The workhouse medical officer was called to give evidence and he said that Martha Whiteside had previously been admitted to the institution suffering from alcoholic delusions.

At the end of their deliberations the jury found Callaghan "Guilty", but were unable to reach agreement on Beardsworth, and the judge ordered him to be retried at Liverpool Assizes.

When the judge asked Callaghan if he had anything to say before sentence was passed he replied in a loud distressing voice: "No sir, but God forgive the woman who has sworn away my life". The judge then donned the black cap and sentenced the convicted man to death.

When Beardsworth was re-tried at Liverpool Assizes, his defence counsel, Mr. Lyndon Riley, strongly rebuffed the prosecution's allegations that his client had tried to silence Sarah Harris by marrying her. He claimed that there was not a woman in the world who would knowingly walk down the aisle to take the hand of a murderer.

The most dramatic moment of the trial occurred just as the judge was about to begin his summing up. A warder from Preston Prison rushed into court with a piece of paper which was handed to the judge. The note stated that a prisoner at Preston had just made a vital statement which could offer important evidence.

The case was then adjourned until the following morning when the prisoner appeared to give his evidence. He claimed that while in the exercise yard with Beardsworth during Beardsworth's trial, the accused had told him: "I murdered Old Fell. Callaghan had nothing to do with it". When cross-examined by the defence Counsel the convict admitted that he could have given his evidence several weeks earlier.

Despite the late drama the jury returned from their deliberations with a "Not Guilty" verdict. Meanwhile the trial had caused great interest in Preston and the news of Beardsworth's acquittal soon reached the town. Many people believed he had cheated the gallows and when he returned to Preston Railway Station after mid-

The warehouse building as it is today, remains little changed, since the time of the murder of eccentric miser, James Fell in 1906.

night, a large hostile crowd was waiting. The stationmaster alerted the police and on arrival Beardsworth, his wife and his step-daughter, were bundled into a cab and taken at top speed to a friend's house in Everton Gardens.

The following morning, news of Beardsworth's whereabouts leaked out and a furious mob descended on the house. Windows were smashed but Beardsworth had fled, along with his family. The police, anticipating danger, had moved them to police cells for protection, but the mob's fury was still not quelled and they went on the rampage, smashing the windows at Beardsworth's tripe shop and at his sister's home in Wilbraham Street. Eventually the three were smuggled out of Preston Police Station in disguise and disappeared from the local scene.

For weeks afterwards there were reported sightings of Beardsworth at several Preston pubs, and incensed crowds would quickly gather only to find he was not there.

Callaghan, meanwhile, waited in his condemned cell and support for his reprieve was made with a petition from the residents of Preston.

Ironically, Preston solicitor, Henry Fazackerley, a much respected trial lawyer was convinced the murder was the work of only one man and that neither Beardsworth or Callaghan were the culprits.

Just a few hours before Callaghan was due to hang, the Home Secretary commuted his death sentence to one of penal servitude for life.

Postscript on the Murder of James Fell

Most of Callaghan's sentence was spent doing Hard Labour at Dartmoor. Eventually, after serving 20 years in prison, he was released. When he returned to Preston, Martha Whiteside was dead. From then on he lived a life without luxury, without work and with a name as a convicted killer.

Eventually after some 12 years, in April, 1938, he died in Sharoe Green Hospital, aged 68 and was buried in a pauper's grave in Preston Cemetery.

Little was ever known of where Beardsworth fled to, but a soldier from Preston came across him during the First World War. At the time he was wearing the uniform of a corporal of the American Army.

Whether the evidence of Martha Whiteside was the spiteful lie of a jealous woman remains a mystery to this day.

Wife Killer Declared a "Criminal Lunatic"

A T the beginning of August, 1901, William Daley, aged 45, of 19 Water Street, Preston, appeared at Liverpool Assizes charged with the wilful murder of his wife Elizabeth on Saturday, July 20th, of the same year.

The deceased woman had that very Saturday afternoon been found lying in a dying condition on the bedroom floor of their home. Her skull had been battered-in by a sledge-hammer which was later found in the backyard.

With bloodstained boots and a bloodstained left hand, William Daley was immediately taken into custody and charged with the murder of his wife. His reply to the charge was: "I know nothing about it".

As the trial got underway, various witnesses testified as to the accused's strange behaviour over the three weeks prior to the tragic incident. His son revealed that on the afternoon of the killing, his father had "seemed strange and appeared very white and frightening".

One of the daughters recalled how she had discovered her mother lying on the bedroom floor in the back room with her head smashed in. She told how she saw her father coming downstairs on the Saturday afternoon looking "very white" indeed. When he had gone she had heard the baby crying and went to investigate and it was then she found her mother prostrate.

Gradually it was revealed that William Daley had had a long history of mental disorder and had twice been in Lancaster Asylum, in 1880 and 1899, and that in-between, he had spent three periods in Whittingham Asylum. On his last stay in Lancaster Asylum it was said he had been diagnosed as suffering from 'homicidal mania'.

A local doctor testified that both the prisoner and his wife had, in years gone by, been to see him as to the state of Mr. Daley's mind, and he had recommended steps being taken by Mrs. Daley, the deceased, to have him put away.

There was no doubting the culprit of the brutal killing but what the jury had to decide was whether or not Daley was responsible for his actions. With this in mind great interest was placed on the prisoner's behaviour after his arrest. He was said to have been perfectly cool, calm and collected when questioned at the police station on the evening of his arrest. All his replies having been made in a rational manner.

The medical officer from Preston Prison stated that during the time the prisoner had been under his observation he had shown no sign of insanity. Under cross-examination, however, he added that there was nothing in his behaviour that had been inconsistent with the fact of his having been suffering from 'homicidal mania' when he committed the deed.

The trial judge observed that he did not think a verdict should be returned against the prisoner, but the prosecution felt that a verdict could be returned in order for a declaration to be made as to the accused man's sanity or insanity.

In his address to the jury, the judge directed them to return a verdict that the prisoner was guilty, but that he was insane at the time of the act. The foreman of the jury asked how the prisoner would be detained and his Lordship stated that he would be detained under the orders of the Home Secretary, being classed as a "Criminal Lunatic".

The foreman then consulted with the rest of the jury and their decision was that the accused was unaccountable for his act. The verdict was then formally taken that the prisoner was "Guilty", but not responsible for his act and the order of the Court was that he be kept in custody as a Criminal Lunatic until His Majesty's pleasure be shown.

Tragic End for Mother of Six

"BRUTAL Wife Killing Case in Preston", blazed the headline of the *Preston Chronicle* on 22nd July, 1876. The report was an account of the death that had taken place the previous Saturday, at the home of Margaret and Andrew McKearney.

Margaret McKearney was the 31-year-old wife of bricksetters labourer, Andrew McKearney. Their little terraced house was in Gradwell Street just off Marsh Lane, where they lived with their six children, the youngest being just three-months-old.

The killing was reported as having taken place at around three o'clock in the afternoon of 15th July.

The woman had been frying some meat on the fire when her husband approached her and asked for the knife, which was in her hand. She refused to hand it to him, he then pushed her and she fell over a stool. As he then bent down to pick-up the knife, he additionally kicked her in the abdomen. The blow was so severe that it eventually led to Margaret McKearney's death. The unfortunate woman managed to stand up with blood flowing from her and she cried out to her 10-year-old daughter, Margaret Ann, who raised the alarm.

Within minutes, a local constable was on the scene but despite his endeavours, the woman died. The husband, who was known to the constable, had by now disappeared. On the death of Margaret McKearney, the constable decided to pursue Andrew McKearney for having inflicted the fatal blow to his wife.

The constable's search led him down South Meadow Lane across the river at Penwortham Bridge. The constable eventually found him in a stable where he was hiding. Andrew McKearney was informed of his wife's death and in reply stated: "I only punched her a bit". But his clogs and stockings were saturated in blood and he was immediately taken to the lock-up.

General opinion seemed to be that McKearney was a notorious fellow and the paper reported his previous appearances before the magistrates for ill-treating his wife. On a couple of occasions in the previous three years the man had absconded, when summoned for his brutal treatment of the woman.

At the inquest, a verdict of "Wilful Murder" was recorded against the man. Though the next day when McKearney was brought before the magistrates, it was decided that he could be committed for trial on a charge of "Manslaughter".

This latest decision was greeted with suppressed murmers of approval from the rear of the court and McKearney appeared considerably relieved, being in sharp contrast to the previous day when he had left the dock in tears under the threat of a 'Wilful Murder' charge.

The prisoner was taken to the railway station and conveyed to Kirkdale Gaol, Liverpool, to await his trial. The Summer Assizes took place just a few days later and when McKearney appeared in the dock, he pleaded guilty to Manslaughter and not to Murder.

The prosecution agreed to accept the plea, and it was then only a question of the defence counsel detailing the circumstances surrounding the original verdict of "Wilful Murder" recorded at the inquest. It was thought at that time that the woman's death may have been caused by wounds other than the kick in the abdomen, but this theory was determined as not so by the medical experts. While accepting that he kicked his wife, his counsel urged the Court to believe that he had no intention of performing such an act as to kill her.

When His Lordship summed up, he remarked that he was quite satisfied from the depositions that no knife was used and he expressed the belief that when the kick took place McKearney did not have his boots on.

Bringing proceedings to a close His Lordship then announced that he was sentencing the prisoner to "Fifteen Months Hard Labour". The powerfully built 26-year-old labourer who had held his head down throughout the proceedings, then seemed immediately relieved when he heard the sentence imposed.

Quarrel Over a Penny Piece

ON the evening of New Years Day, 1839, Mr. T. Ladyman, a local carpentary contractor treated the men in his employ to a number of drinks in the Theatre Tavern and other local public houses. Among the group of joiners was John Alderson, aged about 30, a married man with three small children, and 42-year-old William Bell who had a wife and six children.

As the evening wore on, members of the party gradually dispersed and went their separate ways. By this time much drink had been consumed by most of them and they parted in high spirits.

Later that night, shortly before eleven o'clock, John Alderson turned up at the Wellington Tavern in Glover Street; he seemed somewhat the worse for drink. Already in this public house was his work colleague, William Bell and Alderson sat himself down near to his acquaintance.

Bell, who appeared to still be reasonably sober was sat with a friend, drinking a glass of rum. He started to talk to Alderson who appeared to be drunk and oblivious to the conversation going on around him. Bell then accused Alderson of owing him a penny and when he got no reaction from him, he struck him a blow and sent him crashing to the ground.

The landlord immediately reacted to the situation and ordered

The Wellington, Glover Street. It was here on the evening of New Year's Day, 1839, that John Alderson arrived the worse for drink. Later in the evening he was murdered by his work colleague, William Bell outside Bell's home in nearby Pleasant Street.

the aggressive William Bell from the premises. The blow that Alderson received had not been a very violent one and although appearing to be in a sleepy condition he remained in the Wellington Tavern for a few more minutes. Then in the company of another joiner, he made his way home to nearby Pleasant Street, where both he and William Bell lived almost opposite to each other.

After sitting by the fire for a few minutes in the company of his wife, Alderson without speaking got up from his chair and went into the street. He crossed the road and tried the door latch of the home of William Bell, it was locked. Next he started to shout saying "Bell, come out, I want to pay you for what you've done to me at the Wellington", and rattled the door.

Within a couple of minutes Bell's door opened and he rushed out with a pen knife in his hand to confront Alderson. The irate Bell, who was only about one yard away, flashed the threatening weapon in his right hand and said: "I will do for thee in a few minutes. If thou will step a foot further I will stick it through your heart".

Alderson replied: "I will try thee", and stepped closer to Bell, where-upon a scuffle commenced between the pair. The outcome was that within a minute Alderson had been stabbed and blood was dripping from his left side in the region of his heart.

His wife, who had been a witness to the sorry affair, rushed to his aid and helped him back home where he died within a few minutes. His last words to his wife had been: "Fetch the constables". By the time they and the local doctor arrived the life of John Alderson was over.

Reacting to the information received, the constables went across to the home of William Bell, where they found him lying on the bed in his nightshirt. When they asked him to accompany them, he replied: "I will go quietly". As he was dressing the constables examined his clothes and in a pocket of his jacket, they found a pen-knife which had upon it traces of blood.

It was now some thirty minutes past midnight and Bell was escorted by the constables to the lock-up. He appeared to be much affected by drink and staggered very much on his way there. Next morning, when confronted with his terrible crime, he claimed that he had been so drunk that he had no recollection of anything that had taken place.

Bell, a stout broad man and a native of Kirkby Lonsdale, was subsequently charged with the Wilful Murder of John Alderson, who had been a native of Poulton. He was described as a hardworking man but one who was not liked by his workmates on account of his violent disposition and he had a history of aggressive behaviour.

The following Spring Assizes at Lancaster Castle saw Bell appear charged with Wilful Murder. The incident in the Wellington Tavern was related again with Bell claiming that the deceased man owed him a penny piece. Then Alderson's widow gave her account of the tragic incident. The local constables then reported on the drunken state of the accused after his arrest and the fact that he had said: "I don't care — he deserves all he got", when told of Alderson's death.

The defence counsel addressed the jury at considerable length and endeavoured to show them that no witness had actually seen Bell inflict the fatal wound, and that it was quite conceivable that Alderson may have been an accessory to his own wounds when he rushed forward. If this was the case he urged, then the verdict should be one of manslaughter not murder.

His Lordship after referring to the evidence given, gave a very elaborate explanation of the legal distinction between the two offences of murder and manslaughter. He then dwelt at great length on the evidence of the widow of the deceased, on which he considered the whole charge mainly depended.

The jury, at the close of his Lordship's address, desired leave to

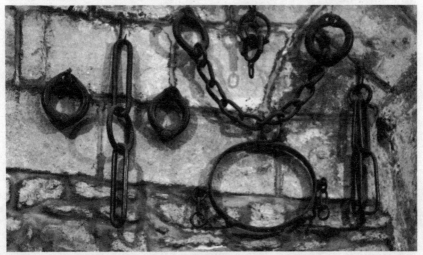

Chains on display at Lancaster Castle dungeons were once used for the 'transportation' of prisoners from the Port of Lancaster to Australia. Long and short 'striding' chains and 'waistbands' were used to shackle William Bell and other criminals of the 19th century.

retire, which was granted. After an absence of ten minutes, they returned into Court, and the foreman announced that they had found a verdict of "Aggravated Manslaughter".

His Lordship feelingly addressed the prisoner on the great criminality of his conduct, and concluded by sentencing him to be Transported For Life. His Lordship also informed the guilty man that he would for some years: "Be amongst the worst class of transports".

The Hanging of Stephen Burke

"THE last scene is over. Stephen Burke has suffered the awful sentence of the Law, and has appeared before the Great Judge of All." So announced the *Preston Guardian* newspaper on 25th March, 1865. That comment followed the mid-day execution of Burke, the Preston wife murderer.

Burke was a 40-year-old tailor, who lived with his wife Mary and their five children, in a cottage house in Brunswick Street, Preston. The home was a melancholy picture of the horrible effects of drunkenness and destitution. With barely any household requisites or furniture, the couple shared a small dirty bed in the front bedroom of their house with their five children.

On 30th January, 1865, the attention of townsfolk was focused on the plight of the Burke household. At around seven-thirty in the morning, the rather distraught 12-year-old daughter of Burke aroused a neighbour and informed her of the traumatic happenings of the night. Within minutes a police officer had broken his way into 31 Brunswick Street and discovered the body of Mary Ann Burke. The dead woman appeared to have bled profusely and over her left temple was a frightful wound.

Within weeks Stephen Burke was on trial at Lancaster Assizes, accused of his wife's brutal murder. It was unfortunately necessary to call the accused man's 12-year-old daughter as the key witness. The daughter, who had so bravely raised the alarm, was once again thrown into the limelight.

She revealed how her father had arrived home late in the afternoon of 29th January and had punched his wife who then fled into the street. Later in the evening she was once again the victim of her husband's fury, as he punched her and poked her in the eye. Then, according to the youngster's testimony, the mother returned to bed at around 9 p.m. with the younger children of the family. About an hour later the accused went upstairs with the daughter following. Once again he thumped his unfortunate wife and sat down on the bedside. At about midnight the father ordered the daughter to fetch a bedstock from the back bedroom to stoke up the fire with.

Some four hours later the girl was awakened from her fitful sleep by the sound of her father beating his wife over the head with the bedstock. As her mother screamed and moaned, her father then ordered the daughter to fetch a candle. She put her shawl around her shoulders and dashed downstairs and made for her 'Uncle Edward's' house at 53 Brunswick Street. Alas, on a cold winter's night, her cry for help fell on deaf ears and she spent the next three hours huddled in a neighbour's lobby, trembling with fright.

As the trial further unfolded, it was revealed that Burke had, since Christmas, been continually drinking and acting in a manner that brought great distress upon his family. Quarrels had taken place between the couple and the wife, who only 10 weeks before her death had given birth to their fifth child, had been a constant victim of his flashes of temper.

The defence claimed he was suffering from 'delerium tremors' brought on by his over-indulgence in alcohol. They claimed there was no deliberate malice in the accused man's actions and that he was unconscious of his actions.

It took the jury only a little time to reach a verdict of "Guilty" against Burke. In his customary manner His Lordship donned the black cap, and proceeded to pass sentence upon the prisoner. It was only then that the prisoner, who had maintained an air of callousness throughout the trial, seemed to realise the seriousness of his situation and was removed from the dock in a fainting state.

During the weeks prior to his execution, the condemned man conducted himself in a very becoming manner and seemed aware of the awful position he had found himself in. The day before his life's end he had a reunion with his children and his brothers, during which he advised his brother to abstain from intoxicating liquors.

With morbid curiosity, many persons from Preston and neighbourhood walked the whole distance to the county town, to witness the fearful engine of strangulation. As noon approached on 25th March, 1865, some 7,000 people had gathered outside Lancaster Castle to view the gruesome proceedings.

Experienced executioner, Calcraft, appeared on the gallows a few minutes before the appointed time and with rope in hand, checked that all was in order. Burke then appeared on the scene and walked steadily to the gallows accompanied by the Rev. R. Brown of Lancaster, his spiritual adviser. Once the condemned man was on the platform the able Calcraft took control with clinical, yet unhurried efficiency, by first placing a white hood over the head of the condemned man. The securing of Burke's feet was then followed by final adjustment of the rope. A few seconds elapsed before Calcraft drew the bolt in one swift movement to despatch the wife murderer from this life.

The final act of the sorry affair was performed a few days later when the body of Burke was interred in the grounds of Lancaster Castle, in an area reserved for murderers.

William Calcraft, Hangman

William Calcraft was born about 1801 in a small village near London. He became initially a cobbler and later official executioner from 1829-74. During his time as executioner he continued his trade as a cobbler. His trade sign read: "J. Calcraft, Boot Maker and Shoe Mender. Executioner to Her Majesty".

Calcraft's appointment to the post of official executioner was preceded by a letter written by him as follows:

"Hoxton, March 28th, 1829.

To the Hon. Court of Aldermen for the City of London

Gentlemen — Having been informed that the office of executioner is vacant I beg very humbly to offer myself as a candidate. I am twenty-nine years of age, strong and robust, and have had some experience in the office. I am familiar with the mode of operation, having some months ago been engaged on an emergency to execute two men at Lincoln. I did so, and as the two culprits passed off without a struggle, the execution was performed to the entire satisfaction of the Sheriff of the County.

I am, gentlemen your very obedient and very humble servant. etc."

The reward he received for practising his skill "in the art of driving immortal souls into eternity" amounted to 21 shillings weekly plus £5 quarterly.

In addition he was paid extra for work undertaken in other districts. He also acquired whatever property was found on his victims and increased his income greatly by selling criminals' garments and various ropes which strangled them.

Calcraft died peacefully on 13th December, 1879, aged 79.

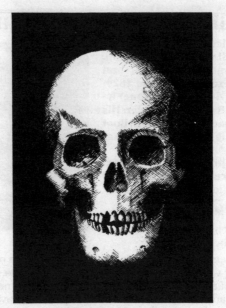

THE END